AN APOLOGY FOR
A MAN

A Written Defense
by
David Marion Herndon

The Cheerful Word

HENDERSONVILLE, NC

Published 2020 by The Cheerful Word

ISBN 978-1-952714-99-3

Copyright © 2020 Carroll Toole

For information, contact the publisher at:
The Cheerful Word
118 5th Ave. W.
Hendersonville, NC 28792

Visit: www.CheerfulWord.com

This is a work of creative non-fiction. All of the events in this memoir are true to the best of the author's memory. Some names and identifying features have been changed to protect the identity of certain parties.

The views expressed in this memoir are solely those of the author.

For David
In memory of lots of love, joy, and laughter

Dedication

"Nothing God is doing or has gotten finished has been or is ever finished, and all there is, is to behold the mystery."

—David Herndon

Foreword

"An Apology for a Man"
Written by David M. Herndon

As fate would have it, I met David through High School competitive golf in West Virginia in 1960. I say competitive because Marshall University offered both of us college scholarships for division one golf; while there, we were college roommates, allowing me to witness his emerging potential.

From that accidental meeting, till his premature death in 2018, we remained the best of friends, our lives intervening as a result of family, children, golf and a deep friendship based on the pursuit of mutual respect. David was indeed a rare individual in his desire to understand life, his mysterious spirituality, and meaning in one's existence.

I do not know who or what makes one a poet, writer, or philosopher, but David became all of these in his desire to capture life's meaning.

Originally the title of his work was to be Life on the Left Side of the Creek. He justified this title, as well as his altered

2 · DAVID MARION HERNDON

title An Apology for a Man. Once read, the reader will understand both!

No doubt his style of writing requires explanation—simply put, his rural West Virginia early life, education, and cultural influence could not be overcome; thus his own personal style of writing, learning, and understanding life emerged into An Apology for a Man.

My original life dreams centered around a professional golf career with the PGA of America, yet America's involvement in Southeast Asia early on in my career brought about new dreams and a new passion. I shifted course and pursued a Ph.D., afterwards creating a doctoral program where I advised hundreds of doctoral students in the dissertation process for 12 years. With this experience, David later reached out for my guidance to help finish his lifelong project, on which we worked for the last few years of his life.

Daily conversation during his terminal illness to finish his work was both rewarding and troublesome; rewarding because of our enduring friendship and troublesome because we both understood time was short.

I have read his writing a dozen times trying to help him stay true to his roots, and also to make his work readable to a larger audience; my final advice was always default to his own style of delivery, evidenced in his final product.

The characters at the lake—David, his brother, his father, members of the fishing village, and most importantly the identity of "the old man at the lake"—are obvious and mystical; and in the final analysis, the reader must decide!

The narrative was mostly done when David reached out to me near the end; my efforts were only to be sure it was publishable when David's time on Earth expired.

AN APOLOGY FOR A MAN • 3

Our friendship continues to this day as a result of our combined efforts to finish his final work.

It is an interesting, introspective, and important piece of work; culturally sensitive, personally revealing, and most importantly philosophically unending.

Special thanks to Judith Reveal, published author, editor, and sincere friend in sharing her experience and expertise; without her efforts this would still be "a work in progress".

Regards

Harry E. Hoffer, Sr. Ph.D. 1/7/2020

AN APOLOGY FOR A MAN

The morning was cold in the cabin but warm still at one end with a little fire remaining in the fireplace from the night before. It was very early. We had had a grand evening the day before and in the night had slept the least.

My brother, sister, and mother were still asleep. We, my father and I, were awake earlier than usual boiling eggs, fixing the coffee, wrapping pieces of meat, hunks of cheese, putting together the bread, the peanut butter, deciding on cans of food and other things to eat. It was good we had fixed the boat, the fishing tackle, the night before. It would be easy when we put to the lake. We chose to walk down the mountain road to the boat dock even when it was the very early morning dark. It was only a mile; so we decided to walk. The walking to the fishing, the lake, was different to do. We saw and heard many things, we were quiet; mostly we saw a rabbit and what may have been raccoon eyes in the night. We sensed today was not, would not, be a day for talking. We might tell and listen for some new stories. We were mostly thought, imagination, silence, and presence together. It was quiet. There was only the sound of our walking and something in the night we did not know. As we walked, we thought almost out loud, "the birds are still asleep."

The boat dock was a light place to see with the least of electricity, no flamboyance in lights. The dock was of rough construction, had been built by hands with the most simple tools and almost no machines. It had all the normal things one would see on a boat dock; the vending machines, the commercial minnows, worms, batteries, fishing tackle, lights, and snack foods. The store was always unlocked. We could take anything and they would know we would pay. We needed nothing.

This lake was a place where people had come to fish for years. My brother and I had been here many days and each of the three or four years before had caught the bluegill from the dock. They allowed children to fish from this dock. It was not like some boat docks that had "No Fishing from the Dock" signs. My brother had once got a fishhook hung in his lip when we were fishing for the bluegill. He had stepped on the line when trying to tie the hook on the line and used his mouth to get it tight. We were nine and eight then. The people at the dock liked kids and it was no big thing to get a fishhook hung in your lip. On that day we had to wait on the boat dock a long time until our mother and father returned late in the day from their fishing. It was a fun thing we remembered in getting ready to go on the lake.

We always enjoyed looking into the water around the boat dock. Various fish gathered around the cover of this structure in the water. It provided places for the little fish to run and hide from the big fish. It provided nourishment from the insects that would gather around the lights in the night. We sometimes saw the larger game fish that we sought to catch, mostly we saw the brim or the bluegill as they are called. I was still young enough on this day to have carried pieces of bread to feed the little fighting fish. The little fish scurried to the surface to feed from the pieces of bread I threw them. We loved looking into the boat dock waters, but this day was not like coming to the dock with my brother; this was not like coming to the boat dock to catch the bluegill. People had always said the big fish could be caught near the boat dock. We did not want to catch the fish near the boat dock.

We untied our boat at both ends. We had one of the lesser boats, made of wood, v-shaped, that had a covering in the front, in the bow of the boat, where we had stored perishable things against the water from the waves or the rain, should the rain come to us. The motor we had on this boat was almost one of the least of motors. My father was at the motor and I pushed the boat out from the slip in the dock and jumped into the front of the boat. We started the motor, let it idle for a time, that was good for the motor, moved it slowly onto the lake, away from the boat dock, into the hollow of the mountains, toward the open waters. When we had gone beyond the buoys we turned off the running lights. No one else was on the lake. We wanted to see without the lights.

The lake was dark, shadows everywhere. The excitement was something. We had the confidence. The boat was good. We had cleaned the water from the boat. The bait was ready; the rods were in shape. We had the lights, the two flashlights worked well. The running lights worked on the boat. We had checked everything. It was dark moving on this lake. I was afraid, yes. We were going somewhere we had never been before.

This lake was not the round lake, nor was it the long lake. It was a big lake but its bigness was not only in its size—it was in its miles and miles of crooked shore lines; the wide places, the diversity of its waters, the clearness and depth of the water it had. The lake had the bays, the shallow waters, the coves, the rock cliffs, the islands, the windy and calm places, the miles and miles of shoreline. It was a place that could not be seen in its entirety. It was a lake that had many places to go and many people could look and go to some of the places, but they could never see all of this lake.

The weather was the kind of the severe winter air in the night that lingers before the coming of spring. The earth, the land had been warming for quite a few days before with the changing tilt of the earth. The cold air had created a frost in the air that was as minute ice crystals from condensation of the lake's water vapors. It was not the frost to linger and stay on the ground. It was a curious, rare, unknown mixture of waters. We could feel, almost touch these crystals. It was exhilarating. We wore the warm clothing.

The movement into the early morning night on the lake away from the boat dock was a beginning of fascination. The darkness of the lake after moving on it for a short way in the boat took on a different character, not of fear or apprehension, but with a respect with doing this marvelous thing that opened ideas, thoughts, experiences, joy. I was simply moving in a boat across the water with a maybe-to-be-seen moon, stars, trees, mountains, clay banks, rock cliffs, weeds in water, various signal buoys and to be discovered shorelines. The lake was calm; there was no wind; only the movement of the falling, forming frost in the air and stillness of the water from the cold night. We knew the day would be warmer as the cold was not the kind to stay all day or for several days.

My father was cautious, curious, moving the boat in the water. An excitement, sense of responsibility, desired need to move very far onto the lake was felt though concealed by my father. I did not know what he was thinking. He was thinking about the fishing, where to go, what to do. I knew very little about those things. I was satisfied to be in the boat, everything ready to catch the fish. We had caught the fish before at places near here. I remembered these.

We were upon the lake in the hollow where once before a deep-running creek had run, shaping and creating the terrain. The mountain terrain had a great number of trees of a certain kind. Those that produce the red berries and have sharp pointed edges to their leaves. The boat dock from where we had come to go onto the lake was named for this creek and these trees.

To the left side of this hollow was the more shallow water with the clay banks. Numerous trees fell off the bank into the water and also a good number of trees still grew in these waters. The larger fish came here looking for the smaller fish. The fish would be there sometimes in the day and usually the fishing would be good in these waters. It was still very dark though and it would be difficult to maneuver the boat and to keep our lines from being tangled in the trees. We almost always lost fish we had hooked, as lines would break with the hooked fish tangling the lines in the trees to free themselves. We knew many good fish had been caught in these familiar waters. We had caught fish here before. It had been easy at times. We did not have the confidence that the fishing would be easy here today and for that matter we did not want to catch the easy fish, the easy way, and certainly we did not want to catch the same fish in the same place. The fishing we were doing this day was different. It took work, new work, a different kind of work each time; and even if the fishing would be easy, I knew my father was not the kind of fisherman who wanted to catch the easy fish. He was here to be in nature with the lake, for the thinking, reflecting, making choices, and new experiences.

We moved the boat into the middle of the hollow and I thought we were going out of the hollow toward the open buoys to very different waters in the night. The bay waters were unknown. We had never been in the bay waters in the night. We could get lost and not be able to know for sure where we were until morning. We had even been lost in these waters during the daylight hours and it had taken some time to get our bearings and find our way to what we were doing. To go out of the hollow to the buoys was not the choice. My father turned off the motor. Our boat sat still in the water. It was dark and very quiet; we stopped. We sat still. We did not talk. We saw the night skies.

As we had come now a good distance from the boat dock, we could see many, many stars. These were not the brilliant, multitudinous night of stars seen in the hot, calm summer nights or the cold, cold winter nights; though it was a late night of many, many stars. We were accustomed to looking for the moving stars and trying to know their names. We could see one of the moving stars, though we were not sure of its name. It was high in the sky so we knew it was not the morning and evening star we always saw in the horizon of evenings and mornings. We sometimes watched this star come into view from the blue skies. We knew approximately from watching in the days before when this would happen. It was great fun to see the coming of one of the least lights coming into the blue sky. We could sometimes see two or three of the most prominent moving stars. We rarely saw all of them at the same time. We never saw all four or five that can be seen with the naked eye, but it was interesting to pursue this possibility. We also enjoyed looking for the constellations of the least lights, though had little knowledge of those. There was though, in this night sky, that constellation that had the three stars lined up together. We did not know the name of this gathering of the least lights. We did not think of all this at this time. Though wonderful to be with the night skies, we could think on these least lights another time in other nights. We were here for the fishing. We knew we needed to make decisions as to what we should do on this day. The weather could make or tell us what we should do or not do. We knew, or at least my father knew, that we could decide, even against our better judgment otherwise, than the weather indicated. We did not know how the day would be.

As we had stopped in the darkness of the night after seeing the night skies, we turned on our flashlights and readied our lines for trolling the shoreline, as we did not know as yet how or where to fish. Sometimes you could troll, catch a fish, stop and fish there as many times as the fish would gather to feed in one place. We had the little boat, the motor was a small horsepower, good for the trolling. It was not good for traveling long distances on the lake and was sometimes risky in crossing the big bays in rough water. The boat and motor were very good. We would not have problems with this motor. It had worked well for several days before this day. It idled well and ran easily the good slow speed. It made little

noise and was easy to pull the crank speed. It did not have
reverse gear. You simply turned the motor all the way around
to maneuver it backwards. It was one of the least amount of
money boats to rent.

On the day of these stories on the lake, I was the age when
many emotional, physical, and mental changes happen in a
young person's life. I was male, still a child, still a boy on the
way to becoming a mature young man. I was of slight build
in size, somewhat strong and agile, quick and energetic. I was
light in complexion with many freckles, brown moist eyes
and my hair was a reddish-brown worn kind of long, combed
straight back and parted on one side. I combed back my hair
to cover a scar on the top and back of my head. The scar had
been caused by forceps used by a physician in delivery from
my mother's womb. I was afraid to go to the schools with the
scar, especially when a girl would sit behind me in the school
seats. I felt a sense of shame, injured, inadequate, like something was wrong with me. In my youth I wore hats.

On the day of this fishing, I wore a baseball cap from
where I played second base. I wore the hat most of the time. It
was comfortable to wear the hat, cover the scar, and not think
of such things. I enjoyed the baseball; it was competitive,
intriguing but I loved most the fishing, the lake, the being
outdoors, outside with wind, water, and the mountains. The
fishing was a different kind of competition than from team
sports. It was more a competition within myself, a different
kind of searching.

Something else was significantly troubling within me; my
teeth were decayed from the availability of the candies and
the unavailability of the dental care and the money for this. I
never in my young life learned the beautiful smile. Here with

this fishing, such matters were not important as I was doing something I truly loved.

For the living of my life I was given the name of a heralded king from the religious culture of my mother and father. I was taught the stories of this king's youth, his bravery in slaying giants, defeating enemies and, too, of protecting his sheep, as a shepherd boy, against slaying wild beasts. I was to learn he was a musician and writer of great songs and lyrics for the people in his community, and that his life was a beginning of a great lineage of people to become leaders and teachers of others. I followed in the brilliance and shadows of this lineage for many years; it was to be much later that I would learn of this man's sufferings, his failings, great wrongs to himself and to others. It was difficult to learn of his temptations, manipulations of others, his self-centered, thoughtless acts in being the king and failing in the intentions of his name, his life. It was to be that only after my own experience of failings, frailties, wrong acts to others and thoughtless behavior that I would begin to understand intentions, meaning and reason, for being in my own life.

We had moved the boat away from where we had seen the night skies to be closer to the mountain, closer to the shore. The mountain hillside here was more straight up and the night seemed more dark. We had drifted to the east. We decided to cast the dark shoreline. If we did not do well casting lures, we could troll these waters. In the dark it was difficult to cast near the shoreline to make the bigger fish think its prey was swimming near the shore as is true in nature. It was different in the daylight time when you could see the lure in the air and the target place for the lure to land. You knew better how to work the lure. In night it was a matter of feel, touch, intuition.

It was almost a caressing experience. We knew from experience a fish hitting a lure in the night waters was exhilarating as to be frightening, almost as being at the edge of a precipice.

The shoreline where we were casting lures had rocky shell type rocks. The water was deep; we sensed a steep descent of the rocky shoreline. We were in a place where once before the creek ran beneath us.

We had been told this creek had once been a deep and clear creek. It had been a creek different from any I had ever seen in the other mountains where we normally lived. Those creeks, our creeks in the other mountains, ran orange, yellow, and black from the run-off waters from coal mines and preparation plants. The rusty waters seeped from the coal mines and the miners washed the coal separating dirt and rock before sizing and shipping the coal to customers. These were creeks where, as a child, I had played, building dams, and swimming holes. In these creeks I fashioned fishing hooks from safety pins and used bread balls trying to catch the minnows. Above the creek across from our house was a slate dump, a place where rock and shale refuse from mines had been dumped along the mountainside. We, my brother and I and one of our friends, searched in this rock and shale for concretions, jewels in our minds. We pretended finding silver and gold. It was great fun. This lake and creek below was different. It was a place I loved in a different kind of way.

We did not know for now where we were going on this day, on this lake. We were close to the shoreline. Just before this I had seen a few outside lights on a few houses in the mountains above us and had thought how wonderful it would be to live in a place such as this. We could not see these houses now. The shoreline now was a little sparse of trees just above the rock cliff-like shoreline. We could see the rocky hillside starting up the mountain. As we moved our boat in the late night morning dark, I looked into the trees and up the mountainside and imagined a man living in the mountains around this lake. I wondered if such could be, a man living in these mountains around this lake, alone and not be seen. I never really ever told anyone about seeing or imagining this man. I would learn to ask questions, inquire, speculate, never know for sure, but I would keep this man, maybe a young man, maybe an old man, in my heart to love somewhere in these mountains.

We decided we would troll our artificial lures along and out by this deep shoreline. We changed our lures from the casting kind to those that would run deeper in the water. The fish were probably not moving yet to the shoreline this time in the night. We hoped to catch one of the fish in the deep water. A great fish had been caught in this lake in the summer before when we had come to the lake for a summer vacation. It was a record fish and we had gotten to see this fish the morning it was brought in to another boat dock. This fish had been caught trolling late in a summer night and caught on a lure that went deep into the water. We did not talk of the great fish, nor did we say that such was what we were trying to catch. It was a secret we kept and did not say.

At the time of this day on this lake and many of these stories my father was near the age of forty. He was unshaven of only two or three days. He normally shaved every day in his other work for the money. The fishing was a different kind of work. The fishing was a work inside his soul. He wore a certain kind of hat that was only worn here in this place. It was a round, wide brimmed kind of rain hat for protection against the water, the rain. It was grey in color. It was a hat that could not be worn anywhere else. His hair was a conventional long and was of a reddish-auburn color. As a child he had had beautiful curly locks in his hair and had been given a first name sometimes given to girls. He had been embarrassed to have a girl's name. The name of a color was the name known to others as the name he was called. Not many ever knew his given name.

He had been given different nicknames as a child and young person as a result of his activities and doing of things. He was clever, adventurous. The name of the color was with him all his adult life. He was small in stature as a man. His eyes were brown, searching as though there was a lot going on behind his eyes. At this time in his life he smoked his cigarettes, was intense, almost intimidating in thought.

He was, so to speak, a unique presence in his prime, here this day on this lake. We never talked much when we were fishing and had always said that much talking would disturb, frighten the fish and would impede thought and listening. It was fun to watch him think.

* * *

We were prepared to fish in various ways, to do many different things; but to know what to do where and when was a complicated mindful thing. It took trying and hard work. It was wonderful when we chose to do the right thing in the right time. Sometimes when this happened, we felt satisfied, intuited that we were lucky; sometimes we felt we had willed this with our minds, our desire, sometimes it was as though something else, a mystery or unknown had benefited our efforts. As we were going very slow in the boat with the trolling, my father would stop his motor entirely, pull in the lines to throw again, to do something slightly different. He was thinking, trying to decide what to do. My father was different here in this place, a different kind of father than in our normal everyday life; all his senses were keyed to every detail, more and no attention at all to himself or other things considered to be necessary but not that important.

The lake was bigger, wider now, growing in size, possibilities, decisions to make. Here in those times watching my father think I wondered if he knew I watched in such a way. If he listened to or could listen to my thoughts. This seemed to happen more here. He talked a little of where to fish. We were undecided. We thought, talked of the late spring and summer times to fish. They were pleasant, fun to do. This day was different. Though we had not done this many times, my father had told me that sometimes the fishing was best when the weather and lake were not good, that it was important to be there and do what needed to be done. We were cold with the enchantment, the work, the decisions to make.

The big light had not yet been gone its longest time. It was still quite dark, though we were beginning to see light from the near full lesser light. It was a light that reflected off gatherings of a fog coming off the warmer-than-air water. The light reflection created some seeing of perception difficulty. The weather, the temperature, was still quite cold. We were coming to the area of several bays, these large expanses of water with this lake, the places where there were numerous islands. We did know where we were going. We knew the lesser light was near to full and hoped this would give us light to see. This was not true in this time. We could not see the lesser light as its position was hidden from us when we were on the lake and the mountain near us. It was not a time of the lesser light when we are able to see everything needed to see. We could not see everything in the darkness.

We had come now close to the pathway of water between the big mountain island that blocked our view of the largest bay area of this lake. The pathway would take us to the first major big area and into deep waters where the original river had run before this lake was built. Down and through these waters were rock cliffs, a very different kind of place to be and as it was still quite dark, unfamiliar to us. I always loved going through this pass opening; it was for me like going somewhere else. We did not get there. And slightly ahead of us also was the second large bay area. It kind of joined the first bay area and had many, many islands; the islands with rock cliffs on one side and shallow waters on the other side. The islands with shallow waters all around them, the islands with big shell rocks on their shores and the deep waters around them. There were islands having shallow waters with trees growing from beneath the waters all around them. We had been to, around, and through these gatherings of islands in the daylight hours. We had even lost our bearings a time or two and were near to being lost. We were not experienced night fishermen, we would be too unsure. We knew that not far from us was a point of land coming into the water, the land being flat and clear of many trees and across from this place a small shell island that was not in the bay area and between those was a long hollow with the less risky waters. We had a coldness, a fear to go far into this lake since we had not done this kind of thing before. We would stop in familiar waters. We turned the boat into an open water area near the camping place.

As we were completely out of the creek hollow and slightly into the bay waters, a frosty kind of mist of fog was coming off the waters. The air was kind of cold, breezy, but not windy; was not moving the water to waves. It was not the mist of fog that comes with having been in the mountains and warmth of the day, the big light coming. It was mist from waters of being more warm than the cold light breezy air. It created a kind of fast-moving, dancing mist trails along the surface of the waters, made seeing unsure and a little unnerving. Our movement was tenuous, though our choice was sure. We had stopped the trolling and would soon be still fishing somewhere with live bait.

As far as we knew, no one else was on the lake at this time of day; this time of year. Not many people did this. We knew that later in the morning the thin old woman and the wiry old man would be on the lake. They fished nearly every day and knew the opportune times to be here and they also knew the places to be. They were much more skilled fishermen than we. They knew from their time being here with the lake in their retirement. They too had their life experience, the many times being together and the length of their lives.

They had worked most of their lives in the metropolitan areas, teaching in the high schools. One of them had worked in the inner-city schools with the less advantaged children; the other was a professor of literature and history in a small university. They worked no longer for the money, they love now the work of merely being here together. The work of being with the lake, the work of learning to just be.

The boat of this thin old woman and wiry old man was larger than our least of the rental boats. It was a flat-bottom boat with two seats sitting up high for ease in cutting their lines and bait. It had the motor for good speed and a very small motor for the slower of speeds and maneuvering. They had the boat for many years. The boat had a steering wheel somewhat back of center for the higher speed motor, the small motor was handled from the back seat.

It had a homemade make-shift canvas covering that could be used against the extremes of sun, wind, weather. The seats on one side and from the front could be broken down to make into a bed. I wondered if this old man and woman ever stayed all the night on the lake and how that would have been a good thing. At this young time in my life I had never spent an entire night on the lake but thought this too would be a good thing.

The thin old woman was not really thin; she was small, vigorous, strong in build, and muscular but sinewy. She kind of vibrated with strength, power, resilience, disciplined from a depth in her soul. She had an aura of interest in others, activities around her presence. She always stopped to talk with others, ask questions, speak well to them of life; their life.

The wiry old man was the taller in build and had a more aloof, serious, determined presence. He always wore a wide brimmed hat that attracted attention away from his face. He hid a gentleness, tenderness; the sentimental nature of his mind and soul. Though others did not know he was this way, the old woman knew he was this way. These two were different, though the same enough to have learned both the experiences of tolerance and appreciation for one another. Both of these people were weathered, dark in skin color not from recent days of sun but from years of being outside. They had not been people to have been inside of houses too many days. They also were a bit withered from the years. They seemed to always wear old clothes, worn and washed too many times.

They wore clothes to be ready for whatever they might do or whatever might happen. We never knew whether or not these two were married; had been married many years, or were merely partnered significant others who had met late in their lives, loved and enjoyed the companionship of the other.

* * *

We had come to the camping place. It was a point where the land extends into the lake with relatively close shores on both sides. The shoreline was very small shale rock, rock excellent for pulling the boat onto the shore and it was especially nice in the summer months for wading, children learning to swim, and of course, the swimming and sunbathing on the shore and in the water. The land on the point was wide and deep and had the under trees and other trees that did not grow too tall for the poor soil and rocky structures.

The grasses grew beneath the trees, as it was a good place for sun there most of the day. It was far back in depth, going back into woods towards going up into the mountains. Privacy and solitude were both there. This area always had the firewood on the shoreline and from the woods. There were rock fireplaces made by campers and beach fishermen. We could stop here, build a fire, fish these waters, be comfortable till the sun began to come. We had fished here before and caught the fish. It was a good place to fish as out from the point, more warm, tall grasses grew beneath the water in the more shallow water and just beyond these waters; the water became quite deep. The small fish stayed in the grasses to hide from the larger fish that stayed most in the deeper waters and came into the grasses to devour the smaller fish. For some reason we did not want the comfort of the fire and waiting for the warmth of the sun, we might catch the fish here and, being satisfied for the day, go back to the cabin. We did not want this. We wanted to fish in new places today. We steered the boat out from the shore, the grasses surrounding the point, turned into the large hollow away from the cold breeze, the fog, the bays. We did though discover less risk this time of day.

It was a safer place to go into the long hollow in the dark. The boat slowed to a near nothing sound. It was quiet, time to fish. My father turned the motor off. We paddled the boat a short distance around a slight point in the hollow into a brushy area. It was the place to get out on the bank. I tied the boat on the branch of a tree growing from beneath the water. We used the flashlights to see our lines. We could throw our lines better for the first time from the stationary boat. We were getting into the fishing. We would be more aware and able in this fishing as the day, time would continue. The water was not real deep, but deep enough, a place where the fish might come to the bank in the morning.

We had the minnows to bait for the fish. We were better with the minnows rather than with the artificial lures. We preferred these, as more natural bait from the lake. The minnows were a different kind of advantage to us and there seemed to be less trickery, less of the harsh competitions. We had the creek minnows given to us by the old woman who sold the minnows. She lived alone in an old white, rambling farmhouse that had more rooms than she needed. To the east of her house was an old hog lot that had a barn, chicken houses, sheds, and, of course, the hog feeding pens. This is where she wintered her hogs, a cow, and a few goats. Behind her house was another hog lot where the hogs stayed in the summer months. In this lot there were the grasses, weeds, and an extraordinary display of the sunflowers. We loved to see these. She fed the hogs with the sunflowers. Behind her house was a garden, a place for her vegetables.

Across the highway in front of her house was a creek where she seized the minnows. She walked the creek with her seizure, great distances to be sure to not take all the minnows from one hole of water in the stream. She did not use traps for catching the minnows. She sought to protect the source of minnows available, given to her. Behind her house, beyond the hog lot and a good distance up a small mountainside, a cave came from the earth. It was a far and a difficult walk. Out of the cave from deep within, the mountain water had flowed for an endless number of years and had created a circle, a pool of water, within the stone. It was in this pool of water the old woman kept the minnows she sold. It was a fascinating place to see. We were enthralled with the place and the old woman.

We opened the tackle boxes. We tied the hooks on the lines. We did not use the swivels with the hooks, except when we tried the artificial bait. We knew how to tie the hooks on the nylon lines. The fish could not see the hooks the way we tied them. We tied them right and left a little extra line. We never had a hook come loose from the line that we knew. We baited the minnows in the lip so they could swim. Some other fishermen baited them in the back and hoped the fish would bite only with the sight, smell of food. We knew the big fish only moved to the live swimming minnows. We could let the minnow move more real when it was hooked in the lip.

I moved things in the boat too much, made noise in the boat, but he said nothing, only looked at me and smiled at where we were. He knew I knew now. We checked the minnows.

The minnows were big; horney heads they were called. We were proud to have such bait. We also had the small creek minnows, both given to us by the old woman with the spring coming from the cave.

We were thinking, talking a little. We will put out the lines with the minnows. One line with the big minnow for maybe this big fighting fish, the famous fish for this lake or maybe the cloudy-eyed fish would hit this line. One line with the small minnows for the good eating size fighting fish. We will also put out the night crawler for either of these or maybe with this line we could catch the whiskered fish. They were one of the best eating fish.

As we had tied the boat to one of the trees growing from beneath the lake, our lines with the minnows were getting hung up in the trees. We lost a big minnow having to break the lines to the tree from being tangled. The night crawler line had been thrashing into a tree in the water. It had gotten hung up also. We stopped the fishing for a time.

We were hungry. We could eat before baiting the lines again.

I thought my brother, sister must still be asleep. They will have a nice breakfast. I like it best here. I wished they could be here. No, that could not be possible, it would not be the same. They will like their breakfast, probably will eat cereal first, then bacon and eggs. My brother will get to play with the BB gun. I hoped my younger brother would not shoot and kill a ground squirrel. My sister will follow my brother. They will have a good time. It is okay that they are not here.

We had the hot sausage on toast, two biscuits with the salty ham, and the peanut butter sandwich, plain with lots of peanut butter. This is the way I had always fixed them as a child, being in a hurry to get into the woods. We had the black coffee too in one large thermos. We had an extra tin cup. I was allowed to drink the black coffee here. My father poured my cup full. I preferred the peanut butter sandwich now. I broke the sandwich into halves and gave one to my father. A remembrance was here. It was warm to eat the little breakfast.

We untied the boat from the tree in the water. It was too brushy here, too close to the shore. We would lose more minnows. We needed to move more to maybe where the fish would be. The breeze was a little more now; the surface water was beginning to move into the hollow. We could let the breeze, the water move us further into the hollow. We could secure the rods in the boat. We could use the hand paddles to maneuver the boat. My line with the small minnow was still good having put it in the minnow bucket. My father rebaited his line with another of the big minnows. He fixed the night crawler line with more than two night crawlers, we put a float on the night crawler line to keep it nearer the boat, closer to the surface, a different depth than the minnows and away from the trees.

We noticed this slight wind more now that the boat was moving. The water was beginning to be far less than choppy. The wind might could bring warmth and blow away the cold air of the night, the wind might could stop, the wind might could blow strong today. We might would have to get out of the boat to do the bank fishing. Maybe we would not get out on the bank to fish today. We could stay in the boat and search until we found the fish. We could do this all day, stay in the boat. It would be hard. We would at least work at the fishing today. We were beginning to do the serious fishing.

We cast our lines in the dark back toward the brushy waters. We let the minnows stay in the trees a little time, then pulled the lines a little to give the minnows a little more motion and to lessen the chances of being tangled again. The minnows stayed alive longer this time of year into the cold water. It was not like the summer fishing when the warm water would hasten their death. The minnows were lively, they were the natural stream minnows. They were not the farmed minnows, not the commercialized minnows.

After only a few casts of my minnows and just as I had made the first pull of the line, a fish hit the minnow and came out of the water taking the minnow. I saw it. It was a good size fish, larger than the good eating size, not the trophy size. It was the good size fighting fish, the brown fish with the small mouth. I pulled the fish away from the trees; the fish went down. It was a fighter. It was hard to keep away from the trees. It went down again. I held the line, quit reeling, let the fish swim again. It came toward the boat to maybe loosen the hook. My father had the flashlight, the net. He was ready to net the fish. He saw the fish; it was a good size, a bit smaller than I thought. I held the line; it went down again. The coldness of the morning was gone.

The gears clicked sharp on my father's reel. It was kind of frightening, we did not know for sure what to do with two fish at once. My father's reel turned fast, I thought he would be pulled into the lake. It had been tied down with a piece of rope. I brought my fish into the boat without the net; it was about a pound and a half size. I would put it on the stringer later. It was harder to do this when it was not daylight. I forgot my fish. My father held his line, the rod was very much bent, a lot of line had been pulled from the reel. He said something about his fish being a big fish. He thought possibly the fish was one of the big whiskered fishes; it could not be a big brown small-mouth fish, no not this big. The fish had taken a great deal of line and was a distance from the boat. We could not see the fish or where it was. We heard the fish wallow in the night waters. I paddled the boat away from the brushy shoreline. My father would need more time to work this fish. He would have to be patient, give this fish time to be tired. The dark morning had come wild alive. I was afraid to look at my father, to watch him think. I wondered if he thinks just now. No, I knew he was doing the thinking, being patient and waiting. The fish was strong, the line was tight, the morning was cold. We were well away from the shore. The fish swam for a long time. The fish jumped in the water. We did not see this, but heard this. The line slackened. Had we lost the fish? No, the fish turned and swam toward the boat to lessen the struggle and maybe be fine. I had the light, the net. We could see the fish. It was big. We did not think it was the whiskered fish. We thought that maybe it was the walleyed fish, that sometimes come to the boat to lessen the fight before a last struggle. I knew to be careful with the net, not to break the line. The fish swam under the boat, rolled once in the water near the net. We could still lose this fish. My father held the fish with the line, then rod, lightly for a time. The fish now beside the boat, I held the light on when the fish surrendered. The fish was tired, probably did not have its true strength from the winter when it had not eaten much. My father put his hand in the gills of the fish, lifted it into the boat. We had done well. It was the walleye fish. We had two good fish in the boat. We held the light for each other and put the fish on separate stringers. They would be better that way, the smaller

fish on one stringer, the larger fish on another stringer. They
would swim better on the separate stringers put over the side
of the boat when we were stopped in a place to fish.

We were quiet now. We had talked too much and made
too much of the ruckus catching the fish. It had been, was
fun. The breeze had become a little wind now and the water
was beginning to be the choppy sea. We wondered about baiting our lines here and fishing longer in this place. Our boat
had moved well off from the shore. We had drifted further
into the hollow. We believed this walleye traveled alone. We
liked this walleye, it was the pike type fish like the northern
pike, the muskie. It was a voracious fish, that when it was
feeding it ate everything. We thought these fish travel alone
except when they are mating. It was not the time for them to
mate, nor the time for them to be active, feeding together in
the same place. The other fighting fish we had was probably
an early feeder; one who left first from the schools and water
places of these fish. It was probably a lone fish.

We had caught these two fish.

It was good.

We ate the biscuits with the salty ham.

A wind moved when the breeze began to blow from the
areas where the bays were. We sought to move away from
where the bays were. We sought to move away from where
the wind was. We moved the boat farther into the long hollow. We kept the running lights off. No other boats would be
in this hollow this time in the morning. We would be able to
see and hear them. It was still quite dark. The big light had not
yet arrived. The birds had not yet begun to talk.

The wind coming to the lake was from slightly south and
west of us. It was coming against or into the cold from where

the big light was coming; there would be a clash between the cold and the warm. The wind was making the waters more choppy, but not yet the waves. The motion of the water was moving the boat. The calm waters of the late night and earliest morning were gone. We might not see the calm waters again on this day. The wind would bring more warmth to the day and it would be an all day cold, early spring day. We could see to the west of us the almost exactly full lesser light. It had well begun its fall and leaving of the night skies. The night skies of stars, the less and lesser lights were still with us. We might later be able to watch them go away.

The hollow into which we were going was long with similar depths of water and shorelines. The depths of water were more shallow; the shorelines were more the clay banks with a few of the deeper shell rock banks. The fishing was good in these places later in the year as the fish made places to spawn, lay their eggs. The water was clear and we could always see the nest and at times the one fish staying in and guarding his nest. We always liked to come here and see this.

* * *

The hollow had the name of a family, rather than a creek. Beneath most waters a family had owned and lived on this property, farming and sustaining on the land. We could not see into these waters in the darkness of the night. We were going away from the bigness of this lake. We were going forward into the shallow waters.

Way back into this hollow were many, many very shallow waters, fed by a slow moving tributary. We would be able to see into those waters since the big light began to come. The wind was not with us now.

This lake was created by men, not a natural lake with the earth. It was a young lake; the fishing was good. The dam construction was completed during the time of one of the great wars. Its construction was finished in the year of my birth. The purpose of this lake was to make the energy for the people; numerous communities and people were displaced to different places and activities related to the war effort. In the construction of this dam, large areas, cleared spaces were created to store food, supplies, and it is presumed weapons in case the war should come to the country. There was great fear in the land. I did not know these things on this day, though I would learn this in my life and keep them in memory so as to not lose them and maybe understand the fear pressed in the human community.

We were away from the bay's choppy waters. It was still the night dark. The shoreline was good size rocky shell. The water with this shoreline was somewhat shallow at first and then became much deeper rather quickly. Our vision was well adjusted now to the night. We were able to bait our lines without using the small lights; they disturbed our seeing and were a distraction from doing the fishing. Our thoughts were more focused on the work itself rather than the light or convenience. We thought maybe also the lights could disturb or frighten the fish away from where we were. We worked at being quiet in the boat. We would not cast the artificial lures nor use the night crawlers in their place. We would merely cast the minnows as close as possible to the shoreline and hopefully work the minnow slowly into the deeper water. We would keep the minnows moving to be seen by the fish. The minnows in fear from the injury of the hook would try to get under rocks to hide from the larger fish that would eat them.

We loved the suspense of when the fish would hit our bait as we reeled in the line. Here, as we fished, we would then anchor to hold the boat in a place to fish. I would lift the anchor; my father would paddle to make the boat slow, quiet. I used the spinning, open face type reel that was easy to throw the bait a longer distance, was best for smallest minnows. I mostly used the small minnows. My father used the larger minnows. My father's reel was the casting type that had the strongest line, was best for casting the larger lures and had more line in the reel for the trolling. We did this to be fishing different ways to have a better chance for the catching of the fish. My father's reel was expensive, high quality. Where the reel was oiled was a place that was my mother's name. My father loved my mother; my father loved his fishing. Those he loved most.

My father said something about the minnows being very lively, that we had the best bait for fishing this day. We could do very well with these minnows; they were staying down in the bucket, content and not needing air yet. We would not change the water now, though we would always be checking the minnows to be sure they were not surfacing, searching for air.

We thought on the old woman who sold the minnows. My father had found her one day when we were looking for creeks to set our traps. He liked the creek minnows rather than those for sale in water bins outside the stores. Sometimes they had the creek minnows but not very often. Not many people walked in the creeks to catch the minnows.

This old woman was always exciting to see. She always looked as though she expected us. She always smiled. She always laughed. She was full of energy, quick, observing with her eyes. She paid attention to us when she was talking as well as when we were talking. She dressed simply, wore the white or light-colored dresses. She seemed to be continuously smiling with a kind of laughter that was hidden in her smile, though sometimes there was sternness in her face and body demeanor. She was a person who caught and demanded your attention. When we would walk up the mountain to the cave to get the minnows, she always walked ahead of us and talked about everything. I did not always understand or know about what she was saying, but it was fun to watch her talk. We had for several years before this stopped to see her. She began to know us and treated my brother, sister, and me very well, inviting us into her kitchen for morsels of food, cookies, then snacks for us to take with us. She would walk us around her farm, proud with what she was doing. My sister was fascinated by the chickens; my brother was curious about the cave in the mountain behind her house. We never knew her name, in fact she may never have told us her name. To us children she was "the old lady with the pigs." In time, she would become the old woman who sold the minnows.

* * *

We had finished fishing around and by the rocky point out from the cove, but within its shores was another point and two smaller coves over from each other. We would try fishing this more shallow water that was not the least shallow water. We were not sure of the depth of the water where this fish would be this time of day. We could merely try the different choices. It was near to one side or the other, this time when the big light had been gone its longest time. We did not know the exact time. We knew it was a different time of day. We could hear new sounds, see things happening.

Very near to us, probably in one of the little caves where the least water ran into the lake or maybe even on the point to where we were moving, we heard the sound of the owl.

"hoooot...hooot..."

"hooot, hooot"

"hoot....hooot..."

We stopped our thinking. Thinking was not important now. We listened. We waited. We would hear the sound again. We would listen; we would wait again. We knew the sound would go away, that maybe the owl was announcing its time to sleep, maybe this owl was saying its contentment with its hill, prey in the night. We knew the sound would go away until the next night. We knew the creatures with the large round eyes for seeing in the darkness would go away and come back again in the next night.

An eerie sense of presence was with me. Was someone, a man, in the woods near where we had heard the sound of the owl? I heard nothing, nothing to make me think this. Was it something mysterious, unknown within me that made me ask my father if it could be possible for a man to live in those mountains around this lake and not be known? We thought and talked on this. How would he live in the cold of winter? Would he live in caves? Would he build structures? Would he have a boat? Would he live in many different places around this lake? Would he swim the waters from place to place? The government owns this land and we walked the property lines. The road did not come to the lake except in the commercial areas. What would he do for clothes, supplies, food?

He would certainly be seen eventually and not be allowed to live on the government land and the property owners would know he was there. My father had kind of said a man doing and being as I had asked would be a good thing but that the difficulty made such an utter impossibility. Our talk on this was very little. We did not talk much when fishing. It was not the thing to do.

Many years later in my life, still fascinated with what I was seeing, thinking through asking questions, I would learn that an old man had actually lived on this lake on an island farther up the lake toward the head waters. The island was located in the biggest of the bay areas and close enough to the shorelines where a road came up to the lake. He was able to drive or be brought to a place where he could row a boat to this island. He had built a structure there on this island. Others knew that he was there. It was a time in the beginning of this lake without regulations or rules as to the camping or staying on the lake. Not much, nor anything was or is now known as to who this man was, why he was there, what he did or how he had done this. It is known that he had drowned swimming in the lake; his structures were removed and he more or less became forgotten. He was not the old man I had seen.

We were not catching fish by the rocky point. This was not the way or the time. A lull in the fishing was happening, it was that way most of the time in the fishing; more lulls than desired. The searching between the lulls was incessant, continuing without interruption except by effort, work, thinking, searching for new different ways to catch the fish. We would try to enjoy the lull. The big light was beginning to indicate its beginning of presence. Though we could not see its indication, a warmth of the temperature was happening. We could never truly understand how many differences happened in such a very short period of time in the comings and leavings of the big light. It would be, was almost very cold then warm, almost very warm then cold. We would stop the fishing; go looking on the lake. We trusted that it would come to us what to do about the fishing.

We wanted to see, be with the very shallow water in this hollow. It was always interesting to look into and see the bottom in this lake. We might see the large bottom fish, the very small fish; the turtles might be there. The grasses and the stick-ups of trees should be there. As we left the cove, the birds began to talk. That is, before they began to talk. It was the talk of maybe one, maybe two birds.

We moved by two small coves and then another larger cove. We moved very slow with the motor. We were careful not to get into the grasses and mud with the motor running. We were in the depth of water less than the height of the sporting hoop. We turned our outboard motor off and began to paddle into water about the distance of the steps of a man. The light had come now to where we could see into the lake. We did not see any of the little fish, nor were the turtles here. We were able to see a few of the big carp fish; they were the sucker type fish. They were, as far as we knew, always in the shallow waters. They were big and exciting to see and fun to catch. We used the night crawlers or pieces of meat or changes of bait for these fish. We did not do this often, only when we had given up on catching the fighting, sport fish. These fish were not good to eat, difficult to clean and we did not know how to prepare them for food. Some people knew how to do this. We did not. We did not particularly like the carp fish. By many fishermen at this time, the carp was considered a junk fish that ate the eggs of the good fish. In the early days of this lake the fishermen would come to know shallows to spear and kill the fish. They would shoot them with bows and arrows and even rifles to remove them from the lake. In some areas there were even laws requiring fishermen to kill these fish when they were caught rather than release their catch back into the water. I knew the people understood why the yellow fish had been created, why they destroyed the nests and ate the eggs of the good fish. We too, my father and I, did not like this yellow fish; though for some reason we did not, when we caught them, kill them. We released these fish. The killing of them was not in us, though I was glad the fighting fish could eat the smallest of the yellow fish.

Far back into the hollow where we could not now go in the boat, as the lake was still somewhat at a winter pool, there were many willow trees. In the late spring and summer, we could go into these areas in the boat. It was a place and time teeming with life, the grasses grew everywhere beneath the water. The willows were full, vibrant, dense and enchanting; insects, unusual bugs, butterflies, and even various vermin were there. The small fish came to feed. The carp maneuvered in the grasses and wallowed in through and on the surface of these waters. They made loud noises when they did this. The smallest of the turtles, the size of half dollars or the coin dollar would climb onto the trunks, branches of these willow trees to warm, sun themselves. We would see these for the first time and not know what these were. We would move so much closer to find out the peculiarity of whatever it was of their being there. They would jump into the water with their fear of our presence. We would be frightened too for the sudden unexpected movement, then we would laugh at discovering what we did not know was merely the turtles. We would wonder at how many turtles might would be in the lake. It was a fascinating thing about which to think, imagine.

The light of the big light was now with us; the day was coming, the skies still had a bit of the darkness and not many of the little lights were still there that we could see. The blue skies were coming. We could see one of the moving lights. It was high in the sky. It had a tint of the red color. It was neither of the other two moving lights. I did not then know its name and later in my life when I learned the name I wondered how it was that it took me so long to see this treasure in the heavens.

The birds had begun their morning talk and it would soon be time for these to do their chatter talk though they would probably not do this today as this was usually later in the season of the year when spring would be more with us. This was not yet with us, though the trees in the water were beginning to have buds of new growth. They grew first before the trees on the shoreline and in the mountains, though those did show the slightest of the green color. We knew the spring would come; the day was beginning to have a new warmth. We yet still could have a truly good day to fish. I wondered how much the birds talked before daybreak; how and what birds talked in the night. What were the night birds? How many were these? What did they say? When did the owl hoot and why? We knew the whippoorwill were night birds. We loved to hear the sounds of the whippoorwill in the latest of the day and the earliest of the night. We did not hear these when we were in the cabin with many people around. We knew that these birds liked the open areas in the mountains. We heard these birds when we were camping or fishing late in the evening. The sound was melodic but somehow eerie, bringing a fear and uneasiness to us because we had learned the bird was saying, "Whip poor Will."

We heard that a boy was to be or was being whipped, and we imagined a belt, for no cause or fault. It made a sadness that a child would or could be so treated. We heard the sound as a song being sung for the boy, the child. It helped to think of the song as a reminder against whipping the poor boy. The sound, voice of the bird was certainly more beautiful than the interpretations of the sound. For many years in my life I would not hear this sound and even when rowing back on this lake the sound would only rarely be heard. The bird was becoming rare to extinct. I did not know what was happening, then on inquiry I learned this whippoorwill was beginning to be heard high up on other mountains where it normally lived; the places or near to the places where the strip mining had been done; that trees had been planted and reforested to encourage the habitat for wildlife. And I also learned that various volunteers had begun to conduct night surveys to hear and study the status and migrations of these birds. More activities to protect these birds, their sounds, music in the evenings of our lives.

The big light now came to the time when it was yet a distance before coming to the horizon but was bringing its light and warmth everywhere into the trees, in the mountains around us, even to where its light could be seen on the distant horizon. The birds had begun their multiple talk. The skies, a blue now, not too light blue but a blue that now still had a hue of night. We could see on the distant horizon there appeared to be kinds of clouds there. We could not see, for the mountains close to us, the horizon from where the big light

would come. The new light, warmth was bringing indiscern-
ible, unknown sounds from the trees and the area around us. It
was as though woods themselves were making sounds for the
coming of a new season.

These sounds were maybe only imagined and impossible
to perceive. Maybe it was that way with many things. We
knew their chirps, voice of the sparrows; there were many of
these where we normally lived in the other mountains. The
sparrows were usually the first to come, talk in the mornings.
It was not the time of day for all the others. We did though
hear the coo of the dove, and then there was a coo of the other
dove, then for a time they did their talk with each other, they
were the partnered birds. I wonder if they bedded together in
the night and thought that maybe that was one of the best parts
in their lives together. I did not know about them bedding
together but sensed this to be a best part.

My father said, "The fish are not here…"

"It is not time for them to be here to build their nests."

"They will come here, come home when the warmth is
right with the water, the movement of the earth with the big
light and comings of new life."

We knew the fish would not be here and did not even bait
our lines to fish. We paddled and pushed the boat with the
oars out of the shallows to where we would start the motor
away from the old grasses, stickings of trees and brushes. We
just wanted to be here in these waters before, as the big light
was coming. It was a nice place to just be. As we had been
in the shallows without the motor running, we had put the
floating portion of the minnow bucket into the lake so the
minnows could be in fresh water to swim then we changed the
water in the other part of the minnow buckets. We would be

moving for an unknown time to look for the best place to fish. We might find this place. The place might find us.

The morning was coming strong. The sky was a blue everywhere over the lake, though beyond the mountains all around the lake clouds seemed to be sitting around the lake. They did not seem to be moving rapidly, going away in a direction to leave. In those clouds there did not appear to be any extreme or immediate change in the weather. They were rather quiet in being as they were, the light from the big light was in all those clouds creating hues of colors: greys, light and dark; oranges, light and dark; yellows and reds of indeterminable colors and in these colors were perceptions of light illuminating gatherings of the clouds. Had we not known from where this big light would come, it could be coming into the horizon from everywhere. Another wind was coming to the lake, not the high or hard wind or the wind making the lake rough or hard to maneuver. It was a wind kind of above the water. We could tell the weather could be strange today. For certain, it would be a windy dawn.

We moved the boat out and away from the coves of this hollow that we had come into in the late night. We wanted to see more of these skies, the weather. We would need to make decisions as to what we should do today. The weather could tell us what to do or would we make decisions against our better judgment. We did not know.

We might could do the bank fishing today. We did this on the riverbanks in the other mountains where we lived. We did this when we were camping or out for the day as a family. We did not have the boat to bring my mother, brother, and sister, all of us onto the lake. My father and I never did the bank fishing on this lake. We could not be still, stationary in such a place with so many choices. The bank fishing was an activity spoken of in a derogatory manner as to people of color or who were poor and could not afford to rent or own the boats. They were referred to as lazy, without skills or the resources. We did not understand this. I was taught that to make snide comments about others was wrong and that to do that in their presence with others was a reflection of their values or their lack of values. We knew good people who did the bank fishing. We enjoyed this bank fishing. There were always many fun things to do such as search for shells, fish, unusual rocks, pieces of wood with various shapes, some looking like animals, birds, things abstract and unknown. And of course, we always had the fish, the good things to eat. We would build things, sculptures, towns, structures on the shore. It was always a challenge to build the fire pit and do it well. We always picked up the trash and studied the old fire pits left by others to see what they had done. We always enjoyed the bank fishing. It was fun. On this morning I was thinking about the bank fishing, it would be nice this early in the morning. The comfort this day was not a thing to be. We would not fish on the bank; no, not on this day. The day was becoming more warm. We would soon be able to come out of our coats, extra warm clothing.

The big light was not yet onto the horizon. We would not see this on this day from where we were on the lake; that would be all right. We were not here to see the big light rise, it was not important now, such was not often seen anyway in my life. We only saw the big light late in the beginnings of the days and it always left long before the night began. We sort of lived in a place where the heavens were infrequently seen either in the days or the night. The days were hazed by fogs, mists, shadows of the mountains, dirt from the roads and the mining preparation plants. The night skies were hidden by the dark mountains, the close together company houses or the shadows of those. The only places to be without, or free of these, was to go high into the mountains or to sleep outside in the night at a vacant lot where a house had burned. We, my brother and I, did this on numerous occasions. We would build a fire and roast potatoes on the fire in the wrapping foil, and then after the fire was out before sleep a few times we would be able to see the stars. I would wonder as all young children do, before they age to learn the difficulty of such a thing, will we one day be able to go to the stars? And then as an adult I would conclude that we would never be able to go to the stars as we have too many less important things going on; but I would seek nights in my life to go out of my shelter and look up to maybe imagine what is going on in the universe beyond myself…and, if maybe the stars might hold secret dreams, and if maybe our going together to the stars could move us away from the less important things.

When I was a child living in these mountains with no rising or setting of the big light, there was no dirt, clay, sand as we normally know these as these were mixed with coal dust coming by air, wind, and water and for a young boy to play in/ with this earth, the slate, the rocks we would, did get to be a different kind of dirty. It was a black, grimy kind of dirty. One of the most memorable stories from my life is that one day my mother gave me a bar of soap. It was the hard bar kind of soap that would take some time to use. It was to be my bar of soap, not my brother's or sister's. We hid this bar of soap out of reach and sight so no one would know our secret. The secret was that inside was a prize that would be no one else's prize.

I was to wash my hands faithfully everyday without fail. I was sure of the promise, my mother had told me it was to be so. I was a very young child so I faithfully, dutifully washed my hands. As time and days passed, the bar of soap became smaller and smaller, so my anticipation, imagination changed to a time when I would ask my mother and tell her it appeared there would be no prize. She asked me to wash my hands one more time. She watched and when I finished she hugged me with a smile, told me my clean hands were the prize. I somewhat understood, though I was hurt. The prize I had sought was not there. Though I probably did learn better to wash my hands, the betrayal, the story would not leave me, my mind; and it would take the greater part of my life to learn that the prize from doing the best, the right thing, is not always that which we have anticipated or hoped to be true.

We had come now out from the mouth of long hollow, the full daylight time of the day was beginning; it was not yet. The clouds that had gathered around the lake had moved along except over the lake. We could not see, for a mountain island veiled our view, where it appeared the dark kinds of clouds were coming. Many storms come from this part of the lake. A wind had picked up and was crossing the lake from the direction the clouds came. The wind was making the waves on the bays, a storm could be coming, though the skies over most of the lake were still clear and a complete coming of the big light could happen. We were anticipating the warmth of the big light coming full.

We knew that now some other fishermen were on the lake as the times so far and during the coming of day are known to be a time when the fish move to feed. We had seen or heard no one. It was not the time of season when a good

number of fishermen came to fish early as the last cold of
winter and earliest cold of spring were still with us. It was
not the season of time when a large number of fish could be
caught. It was a time to catch a few of the larger fish. The
more fishermen would be here later this day if the weather
of the day permitted the old woman and the wiry old man to
come. We knew they would probably be on the lake today as
we had talked with them earlier this time of our being on this
lake. They lived in a small house across the road from the
cabin where we always stayed. We knew from watching that
they almost always fished later in the mornings, would come
back to their home later in the day and then go back again in
the evenings to fish. They sometimes carried with them the
heavier duty tackle, lures, leaders for the trolling; fished the
extra size minnows, baits, lures. We knew they sometimes
searched the biggest fish. We did not know when or where
they fished this way. Maybe they even had in their hopes the
catching of the great fish. What would they do with the great
fish if they caught such a fish? Would they seek the fame, the
money, endorsements, all those kinds of things? Would they
release the fish? Would they mount the fish? Would they be
known fishermen for many years? Would they understand the
celebratory money around catching the great fish could work
against them, be bad for them that their fishing might be over?

We did not know. We did not ask. They did not talk about
the biggest fish. We did not talk about the biggest fish. Maybe
the biggest fish, the great fish was a second thing about which
talk could, should not be. No one ever talked about the great
fish. We somehow intuited the biggest, great fish could never
be caught. We never knew when they may fish for the biggest
fish. We only saw when they went out with the light tackle.

Maybe as we knew them now they mostly were happy to not be working and to just be together with the lake. They frequently caught more fish than they needed and those not released because of need or injury to the fish would give to the less skilled or less lucky fishermen for the day.

I wondered if the famous fisherman would be on the lake today. He lived near this lake, wrote books about the fishing and was even on the talking pictures box. It was exciting to wonder if he was here this day on the lake.

We had come to the place of choice; within this choice there were many choices. Which of these choices did not meet desire? What was our simple, greatest desire? We had caught fish in a number of places we could see. We might could catch them there again. We did not want to catch fish in the same place as before, the same joy could not be in the same place again. We could go toward the headwaters of the lake and fish along the rock cliffs where we had heard one of the great fish had been caught. No, it was only rumored the fish had been caught there. We did not know for sure. We could cross the bays and fish around the shores and banks of several islands. We would be in the place known. We could go to the coves somewhere to be out of the winds. We could go to the sheltered branch in one of the hollows away from the bays. This branch that is known for the place where those without money had lived before the lake was made or we could cross the bay to shallows. It was a place for the disillusioned; the disenfranchised, those who had the least of hope for finer or material things. Holly creek where we had seen the thin old woman and the wiry old man go on a few occasions. We had learned from seeing them on the lake that this was one of their favorite places to be. No, we did not want to be in the place and time where they might be. We did not want to catch the same fish in the same place. Did my father want to cross the bays? Did he have a special place, intuition in his mind he was not ready to share? I did not know; it was not for me to decide. I watched him think, listened

We paused the boat near the point of the camping place, beneath us in the summer months, the tall grasses grew from the warmth of the big light to this place. The grasses always attracted the small fish in the warm months and the big fish would come to find those fish. We knew the fish were not here now. The fish were probably in the more deep water and the water was more warm down deep. It was so that we always fished in the cold spring or the hot summer when the fish were down deep and more difficult to find. We mostly only fished when the fishing was hard and too the fish always knew the water better than we. We checked our minnows, they were all still good, none had died. We had all the bait we needed. The old lady who sold the minnows was a true friend. What would we do if we could not have the minnows? The big minnows we would save for later in the day when we were looking for the bigger fish. We had the bait to catch the fish.

When we would go to the house of the old woman who sold the minnows, she would only give us about two dozen, one dozen for each of the two buckets. She knew it was not good for the minnows to have too many together in one buck-et and would explain to us she had other selected fishermen to whom she had provided the bait. She seemed to be rather selective about to whom she sold the minnows. She seemed to think there was something special about her work and its purpose that she was selling the minnows for reasons other than the money.

My father liked this about her and would tell me later that most of the time her "Minnows For Sale" was sold out. In the summer month she hardly sold the minnows because of the difficulty keeping the minnows alive in the warm water of the buckets and the lake. In these times we would try to sink the buckets in deeper water or put ice in the buckets. In those times she only sold a few minnows to a few fishermen. It was her way. She was insistent. If fishermen came by that did not impress her well, she would simply tell them she didn't have any at that time and would sell them her night crawlers. The night crawlers were mostly for the local folk who did not have boats and did the bank fishing. As a young person I wondered what it would be like to have a job selling the min-nows, knowing the fishermen and all their stories and thought that such would be good work. Each time we would go to see the old woman, it was great fun to be with her and upon leaving she would tell us a fishing story from her life and how good the fishing was and had been at the time. Though she no longer went to the lake to fish in the boats, she had taught her sons the fishing and knew well the knowledge of the local fishermen and those fishermen who came to the lake to fish.

My father admired this old woman and for the several years he told me stories he had heard or seen in how she did not talk of things. He saw something going on beyond her joy-ful, pleasant conversation; it was that she was quiet, sincere, reflective, always sorting things out to find the right words, the right way to do things.

* * *

My father was good at such intuitions as was his work for the money to help find the boat employees among the coal

miners in the mountains where we lived. He was good at seeing the best in the best of people and the worst in the worst of
people. He was known for his knowledge of the coal miners.
And, even though this was true, he did not always do well as
being the way employees are expected to be. Toward the end
of a long career with an employer, he began to not work all
day, go home or off to be somewhere else. Some of the work
in his employment was of no interest to him, and as a result
he was retired early, or asked to be let go amicably. This happened on a Friday. On a Saturday morning he was called by
another employer to come in on Monday to talk; to see if he
wanted to work for that employer. The employer told him that
he had a job there if he wanted and could do as he desired
so long as he came in to work, read the mail, talked with the
mine superintendents about their employees and gave some
direction as to what should be done. He proceeded with some
pleasure but without malice or revenge over a period of time
to hire the better employees from his previous employer.

The shell island just across from where we now were was a
good place to fish. The winds from the bays were coming into
there now. It will be windy trying to hold the boat. We could
not hold the boat there without the anchor and even that would
be difficult. In the summer before, we had stopped and bank
fished on the island before going to the cabin. It was near the
end of our vacation. We had fished from the bank with our biggest minnows. It was to be our last day to fish then. My father
hooked the great size fighting fish. He fought, worked the fish
for the longest time. It was not a place to let the big fish run
and tire as beneath the water there was the big shale rock where
the fish could go, hide, hold against line being pulled and the

rocks could cut the line. The fish could be free. My father somehow knew this; he had managed to get and hold the fish near the shore for a time. We could see the fish well. We knew it was the fighting fish and knew it was not the fighting fish with the stripe. It was the fighting fish we sought. And, as it happened, I went into the lake with the net hoping to maybe get the net to the fish, to land the fish. I inadvertently touched the line and the extra tautness of the line broke the line. The fish was free. My father and I, we both knew what had happened. My father said nothing of this. I said nothing of this. We stayed to fish more a little longer on that day. We knew we could not hook that fish again. We maybe on that day had a little hope of another big fish. On the next day our vacation was over. We remembered, talked of this a little.

I thought…we thought…about our family in the cabin. We had the fish; we could go back to the cabin. My brother would like the big walleyed fish. My sister would be afraid of the fish, thought she would draw and make a picture of the fish. She would tell me what she saw as we were fishing, she would be kind of making up a story. My sister liked to make up stories. My brother would be wishing he was with us. If we went back to the cabin my mother would be glad to see us. We thought all the family that day must be having a good time. We quelled any concern or desire to go to the cabin and I thought they have the fireplace, the old dog, the firewood, the woods, the vines to play on, the different things to see and find, a new world where to play. They will have the good breakfast, a warm bed to get back into. They have the fireplace. They must be fine. My mother will take care of them well. I need not worry about them. I wish they could be

here, where it is different. They probably are not even thinking about us. I wondered what they were doing.

* * *

My father paused the boat again just beyond the shell island. He was again considering crossing the bay or going to
the islands in the bay. The wind was picking up in the bays. It
seemed that most of the winds were in the middle and far side
of the bays. We were kind of sheltered from the wind by the
big mountain island ahead of us and this island stood in the
way of our being able to see well the wind on the bays. As my
father was thinking he said it was too early to cross the bay.
He seemed to have something else in his mind. He moved the
boat toward the big island and away from winds coming off
the bay.

The big island had rock cliffs on the bay side, the passageway to the first large bay at this lake, and on the far side,
many shallow waters. It was kind of more a mountain in the
lake than it was an island. My mother and father had fished
this island once before in the summer months and came on the
lake well before the rising of the big light. They had chosen
to fish the rock cliff side in the deep water and in the dark of
the night, a big, really big fish, hit my mother's line. It was
so big she was frightened and did not know how to handle the
fish. She had given the line to my father to handle the fish. He
had given the fish plenty of line and worked the fish for a long
time so to tire the fish. When he finally got the fish to the side
of the boat, the fish was so big, my mother had gotten one of
the oars for the boat and was trying to hit the fish and maybe
kill it. She was so frightened she even called the fish names.
It must have been quite amusing to my father. I do not know

whether or not he laughed or teased my mother. Probably not. He eventually hauled the fish into the boat. It was far too big to land with a net. It was one of the big whiskered fish, the brown muddy looking kind. My mother and father had come back from the fishing early on this late night on this lake. They had placed the big fish on the floor of the porch of the cabin by the bed where my brother and I were asleep, so when we awoke we would first see this big fish they had caught. It was great fun. Several posed pictures were taken and it was a great story my father always enjoyed telling. He pointed as we passed the place. He smiled. I smiled. We both were remembering.

We had already earlier decided against stopping at the place that would be good for the camping. This place would be too easy and we did not think the fish were here. As a boy my father and mother never camped on the lake. We always stayed in the cabins and rented a boat. Though as a boy I wondered if there was a road from one of the highways that came close to this place to make for access by walking, hiking. I asked my father about this and he said there was a road on the shore and he had not tried to find the road or probably it was an old great road to where a house had been at one time. There were numerous roads no longer used that came all the way to the shore lines, as people used to live in houses in the hollows now covered by water. I wondered if the people who lived in the mountains beyond the government property lines ever used these roads to walk and hike through the woods to come to the shorelines of the lake. I wondered if the boys who lived in the houses around the lake ever spent their days in the woods coming to the lakes. I would have liked doing this.

I wondered in my mind if a man could come by those roads to the shores of the lake and live in the mountains. We, my father and I, talked about this. I asked a lot of questions here this day. It was for talk and to think of such a possibility. It is probable that both of us would have liked to be such a man, though such was not ever to be. In subsequent years, I would bring up in conversation questions, meanderings in thought about a man living here. As I grew older and late in my father's life, the man became to me the old man who lived on the lake that no one ever knew lived on the lake. Though my father never told me this, he did though tell my mother that he thought he was the old man who lived here in the mountains. He understood my imagination, my questions. We talked on these.

My father's life as a young man before leaving home for schooling and then to find employment, loved the fishing, the hunting, the being outdoors; such was a staple for food in his family as in his coming of age they lived through different economic times. The country of his life was in hard times, the hunting and the family garden, chickens, livestock were food for the family. He was born and reared in farm country, had gone to business school for a while in a city nearby; left school without a degree to find a job in the mountains far away from his home as a young person. With his business schooling, he was able to find work in the mining industry far from home in the mountains where we now lived. He had found the lake going back home to visit and to live there for a while. He fell in love with the area, the beauty of lake, the clear, clean water. It was so different then from the industrial mining area now so polluted by the mining and processing of the coal. This lake had no such industry in its vicinity. The river for this lake did not run black; it ran clear from rocky terrain. He would have liked to have lived in a place such as this, though his work and the difficulty finding work here made such near impossible. Though he worked in the mining industry and understood what and why it was the way it was, he never liked the black water. He loved this lake, few people were seen, houses were on or in sight of the mountain shorelines. It was a pristine thing we humans had done—preserving the lake.

We loved being here on this day. Already the cold of the late night, the early morning was going away. The temperature of the day would be good, the winter was more or less gone; except maybe for a few moments of the cold. Spring on the calendar would be here in a few days. We would today have a good day to fish.

* * *

In the other mountains where we lived our normal life, the school and my father's work life, we lived in a shot gun type house that was one in a row of many houses; those were the company owned houses. The spacing together of their houses was close and in a narrow hollow in the mountains. In front of the house was a red rock road then a creek, then a mining shop area for maintenance of the mining equipment. Behind our house was a gravel road and just beyond this the mountain went straight up, more or less. Over top of the house where we lived, an aerial tram ran with motor cars riding on cables carrying rock, slate, and bits of coal to be dumped into a hopper that would ride another cable system to dump the material into a valley, to be dumped to make a huge slate dump. The slate being dumped was filling the valley. The slate dump burned from the spontaneous combustion of the coal. The smoke and stench from this was difficult and was always in the air. It was in these mountains where my brother, me, and the children in the houses played.

Most of the mountain area behind our houses was in the woods where we were away from and out of sight from the mining camp and the aerial tram operation. We were able to follow a ridge line past the aerial tram operation and the slate dump and got to the very top where there was a huge outcrop of rock, a place we called "Shaky Rock" because when we were there it would shake as though to maybe be falling. It was treacherous. We carved our initials and had exciting fun. We played games around the rock outcrops. In those mountains we spent days swinging on grape vines, having paw-paw battles, playing army games, riding down sage brush froths on cardboard, feuding with children as our enemies from another coal camp. Sometimes battling with the BB guns. We built dams in mountain streams and there was a place where someone had constructed a block end cement dam where we could swim. We climbed trees, improved access to these. We built houses in the woods by pulling together the tops of trees making sort of a teepee. It was in these mountains that I began to learn about boys and girls when an older girl, while wrestling with me, tried to put her head on my private parts, and then too, was when another older girl, being my best friend girl, in helping me to build the tree house went into our tree house with an older boy and I was to learn that we could be friends no more. And there was to be another girl whom I was to tell that she could have a coin in my pocket if she wanted to put her hand in my pocket to get the coin. So be it, this is how it all began, my beginning lessons in the woods. In the mountains, behind our house there were no constraints, expectations. We did not have to be home until near dark or dinnertime. The woods were a place to play when we could not be seen, we could not be known. It was a time, a different kind of learning, education; such informed me, imbued to me a quality of life that never left me. As this child, I sometimes sensed a presence that was never seen, it was a pleasant kind of presence, not of a supreme being with a name or any of the hard thoughts I had been taught; maybe, it was a kind of connection with whatever is life itself.

Maybe my experiences as a youth in the mountains with coal mining operations, was the beginning of my wanting a man to be living in the mountains around the lake. I had as a boy heard stories of a man living down in the other mountains for various reasons such as homeless men, there without good minds or normal lives, those mentally ill, veterans of wars who could not find their way back to community, escaped criminals or those running from the law. All the stories seemed to have fear, suspicion around who and what they were about. I never saw any of those men, nor places they might have been. As we were near to the camping place, I asked my father if we could come back in the summer months some time; bring my mother, brother, and sister and do the camping. He said he was planning to bring us back on the next vacation and rent one of the small houseboats and do this. He did think the next summer gave him time.

It would be many years later before I would actually come to this lake and do the camping. As a young man with a woman and our children, we came here to this place and did the camping. It was in a time before the time of permits and designated areas for camping. We came to this place in the small rental boats. I would first bring the camping gear, food, fishing tackle and then return to the boat dock to bring my wife and our three children. With no communication devices, no roads for access, there were risks involved. We were careful, aware and never had any problems; except one time there was terrible wind and rainstorms.

The times of these camping days were extraordinary. A few times other couples and their children came with us. Our children began learning to swim in their diaper days, wearing the life jackets for first learning comfort in the water; it was as though they never did not know how to swim. We floated on the floats, pulled our children behind these with the rope, swam in coves, did the sunbathing. One of the children swam above the tall grasses with his snorkel and face mask activity, catching the little fighting fish with his hand-held line and hook with his hands. He was the fishing pole. It was all great fun. We, famished for food, ate the great meals of fish, turtles, the beans and wieners, the canned ravioli and did the tantalizing barbecued meats. We did all the different types of fishing, setting shore lines with big bait for the big whiskered fish. We got out the floating jug lines at night to be searched for in the morning. We sat on the shores and did nothing, watching the big fish trying to catch, eat the little fish that come too close to the shore for the big fish to get them. We watched the little fish swim toward the big fish and swim back to shallow to be teasing, daring and playful with the big fish. Those were the greatest of times and the best of sleep.

In those times I began to reflect more on the probability of a man living alone in the mountains around this lake. He could not have a place of permanent shelter constructed by himself. It would be seen by the fishermen, the people in houseboats, the government employees who each year marked the property lines. A single way of access would have its difficulties with ways becoming familiar. He would need to be able to carry few supplies, gear, tools, food, and know how to live off animals, berries, fruit, food in the woods and fish from the lake. Living in those mountains would require knowledge and resourcefulness, experience with doing those kinds of things. Such a man could be. He could come to the lake many times over a long period of time. He could access the areas where he wanted to be many different ways and could stay longer and longer times. He could come in boats for extended times, knowing where and how to hide the boats. He could come in a houseboat. He could live in a house near the government property around the lake and learn to walk and swim to different places. He could live many miles away, coming here to stay in the cabins, camping in the camping places, living in a houseboat, and venturing off to different places on his own. He could come from different places, various ways many different times. He could learn to fix places, ways to be hidden and not known.

Who could such a man be? Maybe he was a wanderer, a man who traveled aimlessly, doing many different things in many different places and having enjoyed most the mountains around the lake staying here most. Maybe he was a peculiar eccentric, deviating from conventional patterns of human behavior. Maybe he was a homeless man who worked from time to time to earn the money to come here from time to time. Maybe he was a writer, teacher, philosopher, who came here from time to time to think something out; maybe he was simply a man who enjoyed being with the security of things, relying on his will to survive, to teach him something he was searching to understand.

Why would a man come to search out and find a place and way of being in pure solitude when no one knows where one is or what one is doing? Would he think not only in such aloneness, being by himself, he could find a connection with something for which he was seeking, something unknown even to him? Was he pushing the limits of his own consciousness to see into both the light and the dark shadows, take in clarity of mind to understand, experience something he could not know? Why would he seek such a connection, such a resonance with his life, his existence, the natural world around his presence? Maybe he sought the innocence of being. Could he have come here to simply work and think, knowing well that he would neither fix himself nor solve any great problems and that with this he was content with work being his pleasure and thought being his property. What would be his work? What would he think? Maybe it being the only place for him to be?

* * *

The day now was when the big light was coming into the sky. It had come beyond the horizon and was trying to shine its way through the cloud cover in the area of the lake. The winds still blew in the bay areas. We were in the very heart, place of choice.

My father was thinking, experiencing, remembering. He was not thinking of where we were going on the lake, that had been decided. I did not know this thought, I knew what was going on was important. He was thinking of my mother.

Your mother, from where you came...

She is a beautiful woman.

We are lucky.

She has already cooked the breakfast.

She is waiting for us.

Maybe she is even fixing the fireplace.

She does so many things well.

Have you seen her forgiveness?

She talked of coming with us on the lake.

We talked about you.

Only two of us could go in the little boat.

Whether you were ready enough for the day on the lake.

We fixed some of this food.

We saw to you, your brother and sister going to bed.

We, your mother and I, somehow knew what could happen on the lake.

We were out last night.

We loved each other.

We were fantastic.

We almost never slept...

My father did not say these things. He turned the boat to go through the passageway. We would not go to the cabin. He was a presence within his body. I sensed, intuited this presence. The passageway was the choice; it was between the island and the mountains where the cabin was. It had the deep rocky shoreline of the mountain on one side and on the other the less deep, small shell shore of the island. It was marvelous to go through this place. It was a place where many could go and come many times. We could even do this again but somehow it was fun. This time could never happen again, but remain a celebrated place. We had decided against the comfort, the pleasure.

The weather on days before had told us what we should do or not do and would do the same in future days, but on this day, the weather would not decide for us. We would decide. I remember now in the earlier days of my youth the cold, wet, rainy times when such kept me inside; the pain of such days has never left me and to this day I do not care to be inside; also in my youth, it was my good fortune too soon after this fishing day to be able to begin work delivering newspapers, such would be a great teacher in my life.

We had decided; we had gone through the passageway. We could fish the clay, muddy murky flats, the most shallow waters or we could cross the bay. We had fished the shallow waters before, we did not believe the fish were yet in these kinds of waters, the fish were still coming from the deeper waters of the winter.

It was not time to cross the bay. I wanted to cross the bay; we wanted to cross the bay. It was not time, it was too early in the day. We had chosen to go down the long crescent shaped rocky cliffs that had beneath them the deepest parts of the lake, here the river bed lay beneath us, way down deep. There was always a different sensation of fear in these waters, the depth beneath us, around us was more unknown. The rock cliffs along this part of the lake were shadowed, the shoreline was jagged from the big waves beating against them for many years; they were difficult waters to fish with the minnows. We chose to take our minnows off our lines and rig them for the trolling. We did not do much of the trolling.

I had read all the books on fishing techniques, the grand equipment, the tackle boxes full of lures, the electric motors, the fast boats, the racing boats to the fishing, the beautiful boats. We were in one of the little boats, the old fishing boats that first came to this lake when the lake was born.

There were always pictures of success in the books on fishing. I very secretly envied and was jealous of their success and wondered if the pictures were true. We had seen these people on the lake before and wondered if they were doing well. They had such good equipment to move to a lot of places to catch the fish. They had excellent control of their boat in difficult waters. They cast their lures perfectly. They never stayed long where we were fishing. When they decided to move to a different part of the lake, it was easy.

Equipment makes things easier but does not change the mind, heart, or soul; does not create the person!

For the trolling we did not have many of the deep sinking lures for these waters. The trolling though would be best with the wind blowing the waters toward the steep, deep shores. We could have the boat moving slow and not too close to the shore. I had read many books on the fishing and somewhat envied those with the fancy boats, expensive equipment, knowledge about the fishing lures. The old woman who sold the minnows had told us she did not like using the artificial bait, that such could cost a lot of the money and could convince a person that the secret to being a successful fisherman was in the equipment, the spending of more money. My father and the old woman enjoyed talking together about those kinds of matters; they were kindred spirits. She would become exuberant, feisty, and say things like "The equipment can't think" or "fishing isn't just about catching the fish, competing or doing better than another." She would expound on her views on things, saying fishing was much like walking in the creeks and in the mountains. Such was for the hard work of staying a long time with the task, it was for the thinking, reflections and meditation; it was for intention to observe things in nature, with wildlife, streams, and the earth, to gain appreciation of divinity in these, the wonder of creation. She once paused in her conversation and said the most difficult was not in what to think, but how to think, that took much questioning of one's thought, it was a difficult, different kind of work to question one's thought. It took many times, ways and much experience. Both the old woman and my father said, believed that in catching the fish there were the elements of the unknown, mysterious, almost mystical moments when it was the right time; these they sought. It was for listening to this talk. I did not have the surety of what to do to catch the fish. I, too, though was learning to search for these moments.

We began moving our little boat along the deep rock cliff shoreline. Moving at the slow trolling speed, the wind, the waves moved the boat too close to the shore. It took attention and work to keep the boat distanced from the shores. The waves in the bay seemed higher. Sometimes the first winds of the morning would merely be breezes then the lake would calm before the second morning wind. Sometimes after the second morning wind the lake would calm all day. Sometimes a late third wind would come bringing high winds and even storms. Sometimes the winds would come in the morning and stay all day. Would difficult weather, the winds be relentless all day? Would we be able to fish in these winds? We only had two fish; we would need to stop the boat soon to put them on their stringers into the lake to keep them alive. We had two stringers to enable the fish to swim. We always put the fish over the side of the boat when we stopped to still fish or cast the lures.

The big light was well into the morning sky bringing a new warmth to the day. It was good. We had not seen its rising; that was okay, we had not come to see the big light rise. The skies were clear now with the early day blue. The big, almost full, lesser light had not yet but was soon to leave the horizon. We would be able to watch the lesser light leave. It was always wonderful to watch the comings and going of the moonlight. The times of their being with us were long and interesting, but their comings and goings were quick, fast, short, never enough time. Once as a teenage boy, near the age of leaving home and going to the schooling, never having seen the big light rise many times, I had spent a night in the mountains on the highest outcrop of rock I could find. It was called "Table Rock" for its flat surface. It was in a summer, a comfortable time to be in the woods. I was playing off, ignoring a summer job. On that day it was amazing to be there and see the coming of the big light. Later in my life, having seen many of these and learning more the beauty of these watchings, I one day stood atop the mountain and counted the seconds that it took the big light to come; it was quite fast, exhilarating, a pulsating experience, an unintelligible rhythm and only lasted for about three minutes. How could something so beautiful be coming out of the darkness? I felt drawn to be there in the fiery existence of the big light.

The lesser light was just into the horizon, some gone, some still there. We knew it would be back again in its fullness in the night to come. We did not know the time or where it would come. We did not know the science of this. We might would be able to see the coming again of the lesser light. We would look to see. We could see more here around this lake, the comings and goings of these lights; so here in these times and this place I began to pay more attention. Once many years later in my life when I had become a father with three children and we were living in flat farming and cattle country, a stunning visual event occurred. One of my children and I were tending to the grill that was cooking our food. The child, my youngest son, only the age of eight or nine, exclaimed to me and said, "Look dad, the sun and the moon are in the same place in the sky…" I looked and they were indistinguishable; they were the same size, had the same density of light, the same colors; they clearly mirrored each other. I understood what my child had seen and how he said what was going on. We, my son and I, and my other children have kept this visual event in our minds and hearts so we have looked from time to time to see this again and it has never happened again exactly this same way; but, I have thought that surely many others have seen this and that it is written elsewhere. I have wondered of the possibility of the greater and lesser lights being the same and even asked if the greater and lesser of the people have the same light and it would be good if we could see this.

I wondered about the river beneath us. How far down was the riverbed? What was down there now? How deep did the fish go? Were there great, giant whiskered fish there? Were there turtles down there? We had heard stories about very big fish and turtles. We did not know. The depth down there was not as far as we thought. It looked to us as though it was much deeper than it was. It was kind of fun to think of such things. We knew the name of the river but nothing of its history with the people. I learned many years later that probably its name was what it was because it had been given the name of the chief of a tribe of the native people. He was the second to the last native chief of those tribes to live in this area. The last native chief to lead his tribe had been quite savvy in trading land to settlers, then moving his tribe west before the new peoples would force the tribes to the west. Did the native people know, understand something different of the land, the rivers, that they were gifts and not something to be conquered, controlled, developed for the monetary gains of various cultures. Were they a culture going away, being forced from the earth? Did they fear this? Was their fear of loss why many fled to other places, many stayed and fought in the area? What did they decide to preserve and not lose; and if such was lost would their way with the river and the waters return? It is said that many native peoples have a known sense of living with the earth and the waters as if they might have the same for many generations ahead of them.

I wondered if the river down there was still moving, if the river bed was collecting sand, silt, debris from the mountains. Would there be trash there, things discarded by we the peoples? Would the lake one day be full and become uninhabitable for the fish, the turtles, the life that was there and with us? I did not know. As a boy, I knew the yellow mountain streams, the black creeks and rivers. I played and swam in those. I loved those creeks and rivers; they were moving waters. My playground. I too knew the discarded vehicles on the banks, the trash from peoples' homes, the sewer lines that ran into these. I knew the paper and debris left in trees from the high waters subsiding in dry spells. In the other mountains where we lived there was only our clear, clean creek and the same river. On the creek was a great swimming hole and on the river, nice places to camp. Would the creeks and rivers ever recover from their injury? How long would it take? The streams in our other mountains clearly were running for convenience, efficiency of the mining, energy resource industry, and, though these industries were not intended to injure rivers, the injury was inevitable; and sometimes these industries' adjustments, changes to eliminate problems, resulted in hazards injurious to life and even of dams holding mine waste. How many injured rivers exist? What other of our enterprises could be happening to poison water, air, and the earth in the names of our individual self and tribal interests in matters of material wealth, economic, political, religious, philosophical ideologies? Could it be possible to be less concerned and committed to our self-interests and to find new common solutions in caring for the existence of life, could it be possible that our streams, creeks, and rivers could move again as was intended by the earth? And, learning to so manage this, could we learn to make the water clear and clean?

We had been trolling for some time now along the rock cliff shoreline, stopping or turning around and going back to different good looking waters for catching fish, then casting the lures that would go down with their own weight or design. We were working most waters the best we knew. We did not have the surety about what to do to catch the fish. We were here to look, think, maybe learn to catch the fish. The lesser light had been gone now for some time and warmth of the day was quite pleasant. Along the rock cliffs of the shore I had seen stackings of rocks up the rather ragged cliffs. Maybe some young people stopping there with their parents who owned or rented one of the houseboats had climbed and put rocks together in stacks or formations of different kinds. I thought to myself such would be fun with the lake, the deep water just below; and to them were places to dive from ledges, though somewhat dangerous; that too would be great fun. In the other mountains we children always did things in the mountains with rocks. We laid out direction marks as to where we were going. It was good to leave a trail, to run off ahead or away from another, hide and leave a trail. We did things with rocks building and hiding games. We built dams in streams and sometimes would find special rocks to which we would bring rocks to create what we saw. We always stacked rocks on the high outcrops of rocks to sort of mark our presence—give notice to others of our having been there.

My father decided to turn the boat and go back to where we had begun along the bend of the rock cliffs, he said, to try and troll very close to the shoreline. We began trolling in the very deepest waters to work the area one more time. As it would be, both of our lines became hung up either beneath rock ledges under the water or in trees that had fallen from the top of the cliffs. We lost both of our lures. My father said we would not troll any longer. It was that way with the fishing, something was always happening with the lines, the equipment, such lashing in the reels, something to make the fishing irritating, kind of frustrating. He said we still had the good minnows, though we must be saving them for later in the day when we thought the fishing would be better. I could tell he had a place to go. I did not know where, and I did not ask, respecting his thought processes. Sometimes it was just for him to think, for me not to ask myself or him the questions. This was one of those times.

My father moved the boat out away from the shore a little into the bay. He pointed to the far end of the bend and indicated we were going a direction into another hollow of the lake. We would be moving out of the wind and waves in the bay. I looked into the mountain areas above the rock cliffs to the highest point where a ridge was coming to an end; there, rather a distance from the edge of the cliffs that could go un-noticed, I saw what appeared to be a stacking of very big rocks that had to have been from the mountains or were the tops of the rock cliffs. The rocks, as I saw them, were too large for just anyone to have moved them. They were not the shell rocks of the rock cliffs; they appeared to be boulders from the surface of the mountain terrain. The shape was as a tower building might be. Was a man living in those mountains; who had done this work? Was a man building rock sculptures in the mountains around this lake?

In the now many years of my life as a grown man, like the boy I once was who imagined or maybe even saw a man living in the mountains around this lake I continue to look, to see this man, for I also have sought solitude, separateness, from the world of other people, their enterprises in working for money and many other activities in communities. I have been in displeasure with how things are, with how I am within myself and with others. I have sought a way to be better with-in myself and to be better with others. Many of the solutions I learned for my difficulties have been unsatisfactory. I have sought solutions for internal and external conflict in various addictions, work, religious, and philosophical strategies being in my familial life and in the competitions with others and the being successful and winning in these.

I have thought that other people, some place or stance could bring to me peace of mind, purpose, meaning. All of these have given me peace and comfort, though not calm to the restlessness in my soul, nor peace to the consciousness of my mind. I have had to go days into the aloneness of my soul, searching for the true self, the intentions of my life; and, in so doing, learned it is probably true that many others are seeking peace and resolutions of conflict within themselves and with others; so, the person I saw as a boy living in those mountains around the lake may not only be who I am searching to become but may also be many others, that understanding this may be healing for myself and others. In my life now work is my pleasure; thought is my property, work is the way, thought is the tool, questions and stories are the language.

Why would someone build rock sculptures hidden and unknown by others? Certainly no recognition nor the money would come to him. Such would have to be lonely work, some kind of yearning only in his soul that could not be known by others. Maybe it was a way of telling stories in his life, things he had done, places he had been, people he had known and loved. Maybe he had loved the coming together of rocks to fit the way he had once loved a woman—with his hands? Did he see his work as caressing, gentle, tolerating? Maybe he just loved the gathering and placing of rocks because they did not argue with him and, too, maybe they were teaching him something about himself, that he wanted to become nothing else other than the rocks could teach. Did he think of his sculptures as searching for evocative language to be in mutually, reasonably understandable conversation with other intelligences? Was he constantly searching for a medium for a universal language, a way for the science and poetry, the deepest of all mankind to come together? I wanted in my heart for there to be such a man living in those mountains around this lake. Who he was now, had he been here before, was he yet to be? I did not know.

It was good to be moving in the boat and going somewhere farther away from going back to the cabin. The day was good now. We had adjusted to being on the lake. We were leaving the continuous winds, we were comfortable. I knew the hollow where we were going. We had been there before in the summer months and trolled in its deep waters. In this hollow were the deepest waters in the lake except those near the dam or over the riverbed. Close to the mouth of the hollow the riverbed ran so the water there was quite deep and most deep water went way back into the hollow, even the head waters were more deep than the usual shallows where the mountain streams came. The mountain terrain on both sides of the hollow was steep and ragged, such would be even difficult for being in the woods. For back in this hollow to its headwaters a significant mountain stream came into the lake. It was as the map told us, a long and meandering stream that ran near to where a boulder had been, and it also ran through a clearing that may have been an old farm. We had never been there and did not know for sure. We moved the boat out by a small shell island at the hollow's mouth. We could not go between the island and the hollow because the lake was at winter pool. The point of the island would be a good place to fish from the bank in the deep water. The points, normally covered with water in the summer months, were a good flat place to be. There was plenty of the driftwood to build a fire and be in a good place for fishing in this time of the year.

My father saw what I was thinking. He smiled and indicated we were going way back into the hollow. We would be out of the waves from the bay, out of the wind. He, my father, had something in his mind to go and do. We would be in calm, deep waters. He moved the boat with a little speed so we were not going to troll the deep hollow. I sensed that we were not going into this hollow to fish, that we might not be fishing for a time. He knew that later in the day was the best fishing. The fish in this time of the year were just beginning to move out from the deeper, warmer waters in winter. The fish move with temperature changes in the waters. Maybe such was more comfortable. What did my father have in his mind?

The great light of the day did not come into this hollow until much later in the day. Outside of the hollow was shadowed and a kind of dark. On the other side, when the first light shone, there were high trees and in the top of one of those trees was a roost of many buzzards. They were sitting in various places in there before beginning their day of flight. We saw the buzzards often in flight around the lake, sometime was kind of foreboding, frightening, and threatening to us, like were we to be their next carcass? The buzzards are an ugly bird up close, not a pleasant sight, though in flight they are quite majestic, beautiful and comfortable in the wind, creating beautiful shadows. We would watch them in their highest flight and wonder if they were the great flying eagles. We rarely saw the great flying bird. They were here in the winter when we did not come to the lake. As we were further into the hollow, the buzzards were beginning to move from the roost. They would be hunting. I wondered about a man dying close in these mountains with no one knowing he was there, the buzzards would surely find his body, they and the crows would surely feed on his body. He would be gone without anyone knowing. It was an eerie thought.

In the years to come after this day I would return to this lake many times camping, staying in the cabins and even working in the park system both as a volunteer and employed. Maybe I was seeking the happiness, joy, the energy of mind, imagination I experienced as a boy, and maybe I was seeking resolution, indeed finding of difficult problems throughout my life. Whatever the reasons, coming here provided help in my soul; and coming here would cause me to ask more questions regarding the man I had imagined living in the mountains around this lake.

What would drive a man to seek refuge from others? What had happened in his life to cause him to flee? Had he done a great wrong to another or others and sought to repent from his wrong, pay some debt? What great pain was in his soul that he wanted to forgive in himself? Has he been a soldier who could not find his way back to others or in community? Had he sought to flee from some horrific addiction? Had he loved somebody, and a person asked him to leave; had he failed in a great passion in his life? Maybe someone had died and he too, for that person's death, had suffered beyond his will to continue. Maybe solitude was his only choice, or he did not want to search as before in his life. Maybe going to solitude was his only choice to survive.

Whatever had happened or was the cause to drive him to solitude, that pain may have been real and necessary, it though could not have sustained him to survive. Not to have changed. So, what happened, what did he do, learn that enabled him to survive? Did he survive? I did not know.

We had come now back to the headwaters of this hollow. The lake, the water was not only calm, it was also quiet. The shorelines were still the shale rock, the hillsides were still the rock and water was still the deep. We could see far down to the bottom, the water was clear and not hazy. We had come here before in the summer in the later part of the day when we had seen many turtles on the bottom. They were large in size and beautiful to see. The people fished for the turtles, they were a delicacy to eat. We did not fish for the turtles, we did not want to catch the turtles, they were difficult to land and usually broke the line. They pulled stronger than the fish, at first making us think we had a big fish and then we knew. They could be caught with the heavier lines, the bank lines hung from trees in the night. We did not have to catch the turtles, to eat the turtles, to kill or see the turtles die. We knew of the turtle's longevity, its survival through many ages. We knew stories of the people's worship, admiration for the turtles, their majesty, grace, serenity both on the shore warming in the light and in the dark, deep waters. We did not know how this could be. We had seen places on the lake where the turtles would come in the evenings to the grassy areas beneath the water to feed, surface often to breathe, to taste the air. Sometimes the turtles came to places we had swum during the day; coming in large numbers, we were both frightened to swim with them and, too, did not desire to disturb what they were doing. I wondered if there was a man living around this lake, would he swim with the turtles? We loved the turtles a different kind of way than we loved the fish. They were a different kind of beauty, presence in the waters. We did not see the turtles on this morning water as the light into the water was with shadow from the mountain. Maybe the turtles were not here yet?

My father turned the motor off on the boat, we were beginning to come into the grasses growing beneath the motor; the water so clear they could see a pin in the propeller. He pointed to the mountain creek and said we were going there to look for the lizards or salamanders, a special bait for the day. Another bait, unknown to many of the fish, might help us to catch a really good fish. He measured the boat with our paddles and one of the oars, maneuvering the banks, pulling on trees growing in the water back to where the mountain stream came into the lake. The less of water was coming in the streams, as the spring rains had not yet begun.

As we had tied off our boat at the mouth of the stream, we could see it ran fairly straight until it began to turn and maybe meander further up the mountainside; that part of the mountain appeared to be quite rugged. We would not need to go far into the stream to search for bait. The place where we were was not far from the cabin at the top of the mountainside, if my brother and I had time, or if we lived nearby, we could find the stream and come to the lake. It would be like being in the other mountains where we went many times. I knew also that a man could come in the same way and if he lived nearby, he could do this easily and not be known that he was here. I wondered if so might be true.

In going up the stream, we stopped in places to turn over rocks looking for the crayfish in a pool of water here or there. We did not look far up the stream for the crayfish; we knew they would be close to the lake. We wanted to find the small, black soft-shell crayfish. It was rare, would be a good find and an irresistible delight for the fish. We did not find the soft-shell crayfish, we had the one regular hard-shell crayfish given to us by the old woman. We had carried with us the coffee can to carry the bait in that we might find. We needed to find a mossy place to find the lizards or the salamander, that's where they liked to live. We went further up and around the stream to a place where the stream began to turn and maybe up the mountain. Here the flow of water was more, as there was, in addition to the mountain stream, water coming from within the mountain very much like the cove where the old woman who sold the minnows kept her minnows. Though, here, there was no

cove; only a recess or indentation in the mountainside. It had
a pool of water in the indentation with many rocks gathered
around and in the pool. The pool was clogged or dammed up
with stakes, leaves, and rocks. Maybe someone had once built
a dam here for a nice place to be, cool off, wash off in the heat
of the summer. The water was cold now; it was refreshing to
drink a little from our hands. We turned over rocks, moved
things around, moved moss and were able to find two of the
lizards, or waterdogs as we called them. They would be good
bait, surprise, excite the fish and give to us a little advantage.
We were pleased with our find, put the lizards in our can with
another rock or two with better moss. We were set; we could
go back to the lake again.

I wondered if, further up the mountain, a cave existed or
could be found like that of the old woman who sold the minnows. I also wondered if so, a man could live for a time inside
the cave. Once when we had stopped to see the old woman and
get the minnows, my brother had slipped off behind us, gone
back and gone into the cave. We missed him for a short time,
called to him and he didn't come; then the old woman thought,
smiled, and said, "I bet he has found your entrance to the cave."
We went there, called for him. She saw sure enough the way
the mud was around the opening, he had gone into the cave.
She went just inside, saw him, brought him out, crawling, holding his hand. He was not afraid and had a devilish grin on his
face. He was quite muddy, no telling what he'd gotten into. The
old woman made him wash off in the water where the minnows
swam. Other than being a little frightening, it was really quite
funny. My brother always liked caves; liked places in the other
mountains and, when we would go to the outcrops of rocks,
he would always spend time crawling in, around, and under

the rock places. He, as far as we know, did not find caves in the other mountains, only as he did here the punch outs of old mines. We only went in those a little ways. They were dangerous and there were stories of disturbed or drunken men hiding in those places, and, too, there were stories of ghosts of former coal miners returning to the mines. We knew too the feared, black damp, no oxygen air taking your life away.

The big light was now high in the sky coming through the trees to where we were, this day was about to warm. We left the stringer to go a little way up the mountain to see the big light, and feel the new warm air. We could go back to the lake a not too far and different way and not be walking in and around the stream; the cold of the day was leaving even here in the woods. Not far from the creek we were in a plateau area in the wood and could see a long distance through the wood, as the leaves were not yet on the trees, they were just beginning. I could see that if we had time, we could walk to the place overlooking the bays where I had seen the stackings of rocks; that would have been wonderful; it would be only a part of a mile or so, I discerned this. We did not do this. My father was not thinking to do this, what was he thinking?

We loved the woods; it was nice to be here. We, as a family, were always going to the woods, camping in the mountains, on the creek and riverbanks. It was a passion for both my mother and father to be away from the coal camp, the place of work. My mother's father had earned the family living by being a logger and sawmill operator. She loved telling stories about the oxen and mules that pulled the timbers out of the woods to put on the wagons to take to the sawmill. She helped in the boarding house with the kitchen work of cooking for the hired hands; mostly though, she loved telling of her endless hours in the mountains simply looking to find the wild flowers; the one most difficult to find was the one she said was the preacher-in-the-pulpit. Finding that flower was a great joy, inspiring and enhancing, affirming her soul. My father, though, he was born and reared in farmlands with rolling hills and little mountains, had come to love most the higher, more rugged mountains; those were of greater diversity in trees, plant life, terrain and ways of goings were more difficult.

The somewhat level area to where we had come was one with quite a number of the oak trees, several very large trees and numerous smaller ones. The under portion was sparse with few saplings of the least of trees. It was kind of an expanse of space in the woods. The breeze coming through here was a warm experience. In this place a significant number of outcrop or mountain boulder rocks were around here and there. The rocks were the limestone not the sandstone that we had in the other mountains. Those rocks were more weathered, shaped in variations of configurations of the sandstone. One of the rock outcrop structures here was large and flat, had moss covering most of its surface. The moss was recuperating from the winter with a newness of the growing. The weather from the night air was covering the moss, the rock. It was a nice place to be. We had the snacks in our pockets. We stayed here for a time, a little while. A substantial number of acorn cuttings were around us, the squirrels too had gathered in this place to eat in the previous fall and winter. Numbers of branches had been cut off, out of the trees, by the squirrels and dropped here for their feasting. We talked and thought of the hunting.

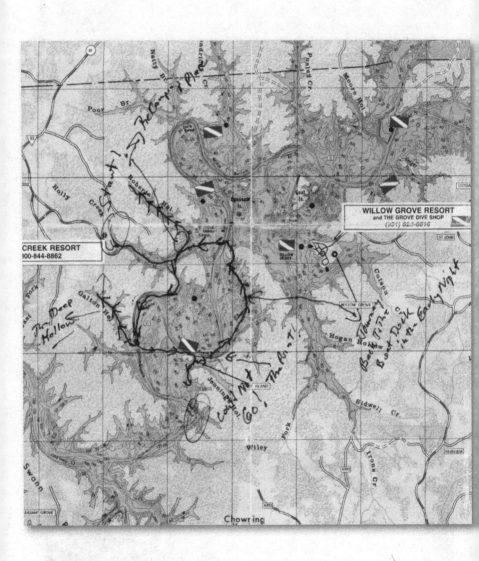

* * *

My father, in his youth and as a young man, had been a hunter for the food, such was necessary. He had done his hunting with his single and two gauge shot guns, plugged off to shoot only three shots rather than its designed five shot capability. He was known for being adept at shooting the quail and dove in the flat country of farmland meadows.

He enjoyed hunting, telling stories of his bird dogs, his training and care for them; mostly though, in my youth, he seemed to simply like being in the woods. For myself and my brother, he bought the minimum gauge shotgun and the low caliber rifle guns, teaching us to shoot, the subtleties of hunting and enjoyment of hunting. We though, never had to hunt for the food. We did not bring the guns to the lake for the hunting. We came here to fish as this was the greater passion at this time in my father's life.

In the other mountains, where we lived most of our life, the hunting was for sport though for some it provided food. We occasionally went into the woods and took our guns for sport. We especially enjoyed the hunt for the grouse, the utter surprise of jumping and the difficulty of the shot as the grouse was illusive in its flight near to the ground and through the thickets. There was a certain joy in the surprise.

A certain memory is now of a time when I was an age too young to carry a gun. We had a squirrel treed in a young hickory tree and the squirrel kept eluding us by going to the other side of the tree. My father had me to go to the side of the tree to confuse, frighten, trick the squirrel so it would move to a place where it could be shot. The squirrel turned and looked at me. I could tell the squirrel knew that I, the boy, did not have a gun. My father knew this, he asked me to tell him where the squirrel was on the tree. I told him, described for him the location. My father shot the tree on the other side from where the squirrel was. The squirrel, frightened, ran to the top of the tree into the least branches and my father shot the squirrel out of the top of the tree. I ran to where the squirrel was. My father called to me to not pick up the squirrel. It could bite if it was not as yet dead. It was dead. My father was nervous and cautious in picking up the squirrel. The event, the day was certainly memorable to me. We did not kill any more squirrels on this day.

The history of weapons in my life as a boy, young person, is/was similar to others. A fascination existed in constructing slingshots, and bows and arrows. Hours would be spent searching for the right fork in a tree, for the slingshot, the right young hickory for carving into a bow. My friends, brother, and I had real and imagined enemies who lived in the coal camp on the other side of the hillside behind our house. We fought with arsenals of pawpaw, rocks, and eventually armed ourselves with the BB guns; one time I was engaged in serious exchanges of the pellets from those guns. And, as many young boys, I once killed a small bird with the pellet gun.

One memory poignantly stays with me regarding the single shot minimum gauge gun. We as a family had come to this lake for our vacation and I had brought the shot gun. Alone, by myself in these woods behind the cabin where we stayed, a beautiful woodpecker lighted itself onto an old dead tree. Close to the bird I sat with the gun. In an instant, less than a second of time, the impulse, the possibility to kill, blow away this beautiful bird existed in me. The existence of a weapon to kill, to destroy was not only in the gun but was also in me—this boy. For some reason I did not blow away the woodpecker. What would have happened in my life had I destroyed the bird? What happens in lives of most who have pulled the trigger? Such possibilities are frightening, gruesome, there is not a word, nor words. So, today when I come across the redheaded bird during my walks or near the places where I live, the presence of the bird is a reminder of impulse, the nature of choice in holding, possessing, carrying a gun or weapon to kill.

In my life as an adult several realities have happened. The father of a college friend took his life with a gun. The father of the woman I loved, after leaving an illegible drunken suicide letter, shot himself in the heart in the easy chair where he watched the television. A business friend killed his wife's lover and intended to kill her also but she persuaded him otherwise for the sake of their three children. He turned the gun on himself and committed suicide in her presence. Upon hearing this, I took the 410 shot gun to the lake close to where I lived and threw the gun into the deepest part of the lake that was accessible and known to me. I did not know this lake would be drained to winter level. I went back to the lake to find the gun. It was not there. It had been found. So has been some of the history of weapons in my life except that now in my walks in the woods or in the places where I live, upon coming across a woodpecker I experience gratitude for not having blown away the beautiful bird and having no desire or need for a weapon.

[A SPECIAL NOTE] Could a gathering of people happen who possessed no weapons of this killing, and being of an intelligence, will, and reasoned resourcefulness, be able to become a model for other gatherings of people, to where the peoples could discover efforts of living together? Would their main interests be going to the stars, care for this planet earth, finding means of trading without the self-interest of the competition? Could there be an end to the need for possessions and control?

* * *

Now, many years later in my life, in memory of this place in the woods with the oak trees, the rocks within the plateau area, while pondering the peace and quiet of this place, the wonder of my childhood in finding such places in the woods, I am to ask, was a garden beneath the leaves waiting to come with spring? What flowers, plants were there to be coming? Was there to be the ferns scattered around or lady slippers hidden away behind a rock or the root system of an oak tree? Was there to be the May apple, the rattle snake plant? Would the trillium come? And what about the deer and bear, would they feed on the acorns here? Would someone come to find this place, move boulders around, bring hard rocks to build things? Would they place those for their enjoyment, of beauty in nature? Would they bring other trees, flowers, rocks, streams, and experience divinity in their garden? Why would they build a garden in a place in the woods that maybe no one would ever see? Would they work with the hand tools, spend no money, and labor endlessly to create something unknown? Maybe they were creating a model for another garden in the future. Maybe they realized they were in the garden and there was healing of some great pain in their soul.

A wind was coming now into the woods with the warming morning, the new early breeze blowing, removing some of the last fall leaves from the oak trees. Very soon now all those leaves would be gone, the new oak leaves would be a time to come yet. The wind was coming from a different direction from when we had come into the hollow. The wind might now be coming into the hollow of the lakes. We did not know how the wind would be on the lake. We had the lizards for the fishing. We wanted to see what the new wind was doing with the lake. We left the plateau in the woods, returned to the stream from the mountain, the stream was close, the boat was close. Soon into the boat we were fine, the boat was fine.

The wind blew into the hollow, the lake could be fun, windy waves, we did not know. As we were moving from the shallows of the hollow, going back to the fishing, the surface water was difficult to see into. The water was not that choppy; it was the movement of the surface water where we could not see into the water. We could not see the turtles on this day. My father moved the boat out of the hollow toward the open waters from where we had come. We, my father and I, might could never fish here again as we had done on this day; we might though, in an evening time of the warm weather and quiet waters, come back and look for the turtles. We could always catch the lizards again. We had not found the crayfish in the mountain stream; the crayfish did not live in the mountain streams like they lived in the mountain streams in the other mountains. I thought maybe the crayfish lived in the lake here; the crayfish are a good food for the fish.

As we were leaving and near the mouth of the deep hollow, the crows were flying around now in various places away from each other. Earlier in the day as we came into the hollow, they were caw-cawing, making a racket with endless unknown talk; maybe they were telling about their plans for the day. They were quiet now and only could be heard now and then.

A distant caw; maybe without talk they were just doing their work in search of food. I wondered if they had a plan for letting the others know if one happened onto a dead animal, too much for one. I knew they would only be gathering again in the evening unless they were threatened by the hawk or if they wanted to harass a hawk away from its prey. They were good at this, getting together against the birds of prey. I had seen this once when a hawk had taken a frog by the shore of a creek. They were relentless in annoying the hawk as it tried to eat the frog. Several crows came around the hawk. I wondered why the hawk did not just fly away with the small frog. The crows were persistent, tenacious with talk, chatter, and movement. The hawk finally gave up, dropped the frog, went away knowing the crows would not stop their effort and certainly the hawk did not know how many more crows would come.

We had come out of the long deep hollow to its mouth, its beginning. A decision was to be made. The long crescent shaped rock cliffs were there, the way back to the cabin, the bay was there to maybe cross and stay in the day with the fishing. It was now this late in the morning, but the big light had a ways to go before being straight up in the sky. The skies were the clear, pale light blue with no signs of clouds. We could tell the wind was up from the time when we had gone into the hollow. We could not as yet see the bay, how the wind was with the water. The waves with our boat now were more than earlier in the day. We knew the water could be rough when we decided.

My father slowed the boat to almost idle, the waves against us held the boat near stationary. My father pointed to the small shell island. I thought maybe we would go there to fish, a place to meet to make the decision. My father needed time to decide whether or not to cross the bay. He moved the boat to near the island. The water was too deep for the anchor to hold the boat. We did not want to get out of the boat again onto the bank, we did not want to bank fish. We knew the fishing would be difficult here. We could not see the entire bay. We knew that going back to the cabin would be going with the waves, treacherous in the little boat. We knew that crossing the bay would be going against the waves. We positioned the boat better against the waves. My father needed time to decide whether or not to cross the bay. As the boat idled we prepared our lines for the fishing here—weighted our lines to get the minnows down into the deeper water. We baited our lines with the fish minnows. In casting our lines and with the lines in the water I could tell my father had decided that he wanted to cross the bay but he had a fear. It was not a fear for himself; it was a fear for me. He was thinking again and I was watching. I could not see his thoughts. I just knew he was weighing things, sorting his fears, his courage around. It was a difficult thinking time—the right thing to do. He sensed, intuited that once the decision was made, he would not turn back. The time made us hungry. We opened the small Vienna Sausage can. We had no crackers. This was not a time, a place for crackers. This was a place, time of just out-of-the-cans.

In this time, this place somehow within us, in what we were doing and how we were doing this, it was decided we would cross the bay. We brought in our lines, secured our life jackets, fixed things in the little boat, turned the motor to close the half throttle. We would go slow, steady, a little way out from the shelter of the island, against the waves into the bay.

The bay area we had to cross was near the deepest bay areas on this lake. It gathered a significant amount of wind on this day and turned the water up into the high diving white caps. As we began to cross, my father pointed to an island across the bay saying such would be a good place to be. It was the shortest distance to go to another part of the lake. The winds were such that we could move against the waves, which was best in the little boat. We had to go slow in the little boat. We could not cut through the waves, as could those in the more powerful, expensive boats. We did not know what the waves would be like in the middle of the bay. We knew it would not be good to turn back and go with the waves.

I do not know what made my father decide to cross the bay; maybe it was just that he wanted to stay with the day. He seemed confident. I was somewhat frightened and remember thinking about the difficulty of swimming to a shore, even with our life jackets, if the boat should be overturned. I did not have any reason to think this would happen except for the fear. I did not see this fear in my father's face or eyes; he had more presence with the water, the wind, the waves. He had more experience and loved being in the wind, the waves.

The day was good, there was an intensity of warmth coming from the big light and the winds no longer blew cold in the early part of the day. The big light and the winds were doing a different thing. The day promised to be a good day without the rain, the cold winds. We did not know for sure what the winds could do, or bring. We knew the winds were most always strong in this part of the day on the lake and that sometimes they subsided, and we decided to leave for the day. We knew, too, that some days the wind was relentless, ruthlessly staying an entire day on, with the lake. The wind, the lake being rough, could stay all day giving us inexplicably, inexorable conflict with our most hopeful desires. We knew this happened some days.

Coming to the middle of the bay and just beyond the waves were the splashing sprays of water into the boat. We were sort of down in the boat getting wet. The big light was warm now; the spraying waters did not bother us. As we approached close to the island, the mountains and the island ahead took some of the strength, movement out of the wind. The wind did not subside; it simply lessened in the place where we were going. The wind began to be more embracing, soothing, and inviting us to be on the lake. The wind seemed to be more with us than against us. We had moved beyond the big dangerous place in the bay.

We had crossed the bay the shortest way. We had come through a difficult time. We were confident to be in this place. We stopped our boat on the deep side of the island, close to the straight up and down rock cliff shore. We used our oars to hold our boat a short distance from the shore.

We hoped to fish toward the shore and also out into the deeper water. The river ran beneath us here and the water was very deep. Being on the mountainous side of the island kept the wind, waves from moving us around too much. Now, to us a tree had fallen into the lake from the mountainside. My father talked that maybe we could drift to there. It would be a good place to fish. We did not want to run the motor on the boat to this place. We wanted to drift quiet to this place.

This island was the first of gatherings of many islands in the main bay area of this lake. The other side of this island had the small shell shoreline; the depth of the water though deep was gradual. It was a shoreline good for the bank fishing, swimming, tying up a boat and pulling onto the shore. We did not desire to be there on this day as direct wind was there. We wanted to be out of the wind for a time. The island on the other side was a good place for the camping, bank fishing as the terrain had grassy areas, few trees, and numerous somewhat level areas. Almost all the islands on this lake had good places for the camping, building fires, and enjoying being with the lake. And, for many years many people would do this; and I in many later years would return to this lake for camping with the woman in my life and our children. These were good times.

Now in the later years of my life I have wondered if a man living on this lake in the mountains would come to these camping areas. What would he find? Why would he come to see these places? Would he pick up and gather fresh debris left? Would he work on camping areas, clean and build fire pits? Would he do this work for no money? Why would he do such a thing? How did he get to these many places? Did he swim from the mountain shores to the islands? Did he swim across the bays in the night? How did he swim to not be seen? Did he swim like a turtle? Or an alligator to be beneath the water? Did he put the finds in conspicuous places to be seen and picked up by most in the big boats? Did he find things of value and leave so these could be easily found? Did he find things that he could use for his own fishing? Did he keep and collect useless things for an unknown pleasure? Did he find tools or things for use in the places where he slept, relaxed, and ate his meals? He must have learned to live with the least of things. Maybe he was keen on learning unknown skills of resourcefulness. Why would he do such a thing?

The fishing here now with the island we believed would be good. We wanted, we needed the fishing to be good. We had fished quite a few times in varieties of ways. We had only the two fish from long before daybreak. We had the good bait; we had done the good work of staying with the lake. We would use the bait of our minnows and vary the sizes with our lines. My father cast the large minnows. I cast the small minnows. We let one small minnow drift on a line with a tied down rod from the boat. We did the same with a large minnow.

We loved fishing with the minnows. We had confidence with this bait. We loved the old woman who sold the minnows. We loved her work and how she cared for the minnows. We knew she would be thinking about us. Did she pray for us? Did she pray a blessing on her minnows for good catches? Why did she work so hard to provide these for a few fishermen? Did she dream that the great fish would be caught on her bait? What was in her mind as she walked in the creek, when she carried the minnows up the mountain to this place of the cover? Why didn't she build an aeration tank near her house so as to minimize the work and sell more minnows? What was in her mind as she did what she did?

I have never lost memory of this woman. Her memory grows, changes, she comes and goes with new meanings. She hangs around in my soul teaching, entreating me to something else.

A number of years after the times of fishing with my father on this lake I returned to the lake to fish; checked to see if the old woman with the pigs who sold the minnows was still there. Found that the house was still there. No one lived there. I assumed she had died. Most of the windows were boarded up. I checked the creek, set a minnow trap but could not bring myself to go out of this property to see the cove again. In later years of my life, being more intrigued about who this woman was and what else could be known about her life, I was to learn that when we knew her she was a widow whose husband had been a blacksmith, a worker in creating hand tools, and artistic things; that she had had two sons and they no longer lived in the area. She had been primarily a mother, wife, farming person and caretaker of the property. I also learned she was a writer submitting poetry, fishing stories, philosophical quips and little essays to the local weekly newspaper. She was a proponent of a self-made system of ideas around her understanding about what love is or might be in the human experience. She did not cite, claim any authorities to support her thought, and in her thought used mostly questions and stories to convey what she believed, thought might be true. She kind of thought that no way by itself could make things better and that somehow different approaches could find a way. She was perceived by some to be peculiar, eccentric, out of the ordinary and even unapproachable. Some thought she was an unbeliever because her questions were annoying to many people of faith. She sort of played games with herself in her mind and took, found humor in many principles of belief. Maybe she was helping herself and others in learning not what to think but how to think. Intrigued upon learning these things I asked about where a gathering of her writing might be and was told they were probably boxed up somewhere and the relatives or people who had them would probably be suspicious of anyone who wanted to read these; so I released the possibility of ever reading these.

Her writings are boxed up in the house, kept by relatives. Her philosophy of love, the embrace... Later in my life I had sought to see these writings and might use them in my memory of her but those entrusted with them did not want to share them with a stranger outside the family…it is unknown the state of those now.

As we were here with the island, the winds began to move, the waves and turning over white caps in the bay area were greater and more treacherous, marked with deception, unforeseen hazards. They were dangerous; we had gained success in crossing the bay in a fortunate time. The wind though greater seemed to be lower to the lake, lambasting the other side of the island. The waves starting again out there held us toward the island. It was how wind and waves sometimes work with an island. We were in a content place.

The two fish we had caught were still alive, having kept them on the separate stringers in separate buckets of water. We desired the fish to live till it was time to kill the fish, fillet them for the ice, freezing, or preparing them for our food. The fish had had good time in this water. The smaller fish always survived the catching but the larger fish seemed to suffer most. We might have to kill the large fish from the morning's catch. We could fillet the fish and put them in our ice chest.

We checked our minnows. They were swimming low in their buckets. They liked the cold early spring water; they liked the fresh water we always kept in their buckets. They were not coming to the top to find oxygen as they sometimes did in the warm summer water. It was always difficult fishing the minnows in the warm weather. We tried many things in the warm waters such as ice in the buckets, changing the water more frequently, sinking the buckets into deeper water, tying the buckets on tree limbs out from the shore; these worked best, but nothing worked well. The fishing with minnows in the summer was hard. Our minnows were good now in the cold water.

We baited four lines; two for drifting with the boat, two for casting with the weights to take the fish down slowly. We did not think the fish would be near the surface in this weather in this time of year. We were hopeful with the small minnows, as we know sometimes the big fighting fish would take the small minnows first, wetting its appetite before the spring foraging for food. We knew the small fighting fish, not knowing better, would hit the big minnows with their youthful aggressions. We did suspect that maybe the biggest fighting fish could or would be caught on the big minnow. We did not know for sure. We were just working our odds as best we knew. We knew we were not the best of the fishermen, but we were there with them trying in the most difficult of times.

We had been here on the sheltered side of the island a long time, the fishing was not good here. This was not the place to be. We did not know the place of the fish, where the fish were on this day. We did not know how the fish were thinking, moving. Did the fish think? They were after food, wary of danger. We knew the fish stay in similar temperatures of water, moved at certain times of the day and night. We knew that sometimes the catching of fish was easy, sometimes almost impossible. We knew the big fish were caught in difficult times; that the hard-working fishermen did better than the lazy fishermen. These were those who fished in the cold windy weather, the very cold weather, late into the night and in the earliest parts of the day. Today, were the fish asleep in the bays, were they hidden beneath rocks, would they be coming to the shorelines on this day, was the big light warming and winds. inviting the fish from the slumber of ease? We knew what the fish did in the patterns of seasons. This was not one of the patterns of seasons. This was a difficult, extreme time to find the fish. We, or at least I, did not know what to do. We were betwixt nothing happening and the need to search for what the fish were doing. Might be we would have to just be lucky. We knew earlier that luck was not going to just come to us.

Another kind of wind was coming. This was not the wind staying all day, staying the same and going away at this end of the day. This was more wind, moving faster in varied directions with greater warmth from the big light. It was a wind that could bring a storm. It was a wind, an enjoyable place to be. We had grown uneasy, dissatisfied with the stationary fishing. We wanted to see what this new wind was doing.

My father wanted to move; he had that look about him. The bay we had crossed was showing the turning over white caps. We could not go back across the bay as such now would be going with the waves and could be dangerous in the little boat. We could, though, go in short distances against the waves to find another place to fish and see how the weather was going to be. We could try the wind. We gathered the stringer fish we had caught in the morning and put them in containers of water in the back so they could live. We used our cooler full of water for the big fish and a bucket with water for the small fish. We always tried to keep the fish alive. We changed the water in the minnow buckets, brought in our lines and the anchor, we were ready to move.

As we moved the boat away from the island, from the shelter, from the wind place, to go between the island and the mountainous shoreline, the wind was more than we had known, or thought. Sometimes we would get down into a small place on the lake and encounter more difficulty or roughness than was true on another place on the lake and this was on the waters where we were going. The waves were higher, more whitecaps than we had seen on this day. The waves did not threaten us. They would be troublesome in the fishing. We did not mind this now. We moved the boat into the waves farther and farther from the boat dock.

Before coming to the lake this time to fish my father had told me that in the previous winter, he had had a dream about the great fighting fish and where it might be located. It was in a place we had never fished as the place was a long distance from the boat docks when we came during the vacation times. It just seemed like a place that was too far away in a little boat with all the other priorities and activities we desired. As we traveled from the sunny side up island to go between the island and the mountain shorelines, my father had the look about him that he wanted to go to the place. I was ready, excited. He was nervous.

The dream was that in the earliest days of the lake, not long after the lake had been filled to capacity, there had been a year or so that young fighting fish were swimming the new shores up the lake. All of a sudden, the young fish that had been swimming in the river with plenty of food in small places were now in a big lake with miles and miles of water. The dream was that in the darkness of a night without the lesser light or even least of the lights, a huge section of the mountainside with great rocks broke loose from the mountain into the lake; the young fish had been there and barely escaped the avalanche of rocks. The event had frightened the fish, set in motion a fear for a long time. So, for a good time the fish slipped away from that part of the lake but in time the fish returned to see the place again and since nothing similar had happened to the fish again, the fish found the place to be a wonderful place to be, a place to swim and hide from their prey.

The place too had changed in water temperature, with different experiences of light, was unknown by fishermen and the gatherings or frequencies of their boats. So, the fish had found peace out of their fear. The dream was that if fishermen could find the place it might be a good place to catch the great fighting fish. My father was not sure he wanted to catch the great fighting fish. I wanted to catch the great fighting fish, but I would be frightened. We knew for sure that we wanted to catch the big fish, to catch for good eating, to be known as good fishermen. We loved the fishing. We loved to eat the fish. We wanted to be the best or at least among the best of fishermen.

Why did we search to catch and land the great fish? What was this great fish? Was there a great fish? What drove us to achieve or be the best? What would we do if we caught the great fish? Would we mount the fish? Why would we seek fame, the money with endorsing the methods of catching the great fish? Maybe the great fish should not be trophied or recorded as the great fish. The truth is that a great fish was to be caught by a lone fisherman trolling in the late dark nights of a summer in this lake, the exact place to never be known; maybe this great fish was the young fish that had been in my father's dream. The fisherman who caught the fish trophied the fish and gained fame. It is also true after his fame became established as a record, other great fish of record size not of greater weight but near to such were caught. As true controversy grew it became known that maybe a boat dock owner to gain advantage from being brought in to his dock may have stuffed nuts and bolts in the gullet of the fish to raise the weight of the fish. For whatever is true that gain and fame did happen but around this also came controversy, jealously, turmoil, undermining to the fish or the fishermen. Maybe if a great fish is caught it may be pictured for storytelling, memory, and writing up versions of searching to catch the great fish. Maybe the fish should be eaten for nourishment and continuing the search for new stories, efforts.

Having gone a far distance on the lake, my father's plan was to fish our minnows from the boat through several long sequences of rock cliff shorelines. We could also cast the shorelines with deep running lures and maximize our chances of a catch. As we were fishing in this way, the winds were picking up and father was looking further up the lake to where he wanted to go. I could tell he had a place he wanted to be, a new intuition where the great catch might be, or would be, and as the winds were now bringing clouds or more specifically not clouds everywhere but one dark cloud with a great deal of wind. Most of the skies were still clear, though this could have brought the threat of a storm. We did not want to leave our effort; maybe we could wait out this wind that might take this storm away.

We anchored our boat offshore in the deep water. The anchor on our rope barely reaching the bottom and was not real secure in holding the boat. The wind became more and several times we had to pull the anchor, start the motor on the boat and move away from the shore. The wind, the waves were too much for the boat to be against the shore. The boat could be punctured by the rocky shore. We had to do something, go to another place. There was no place to put our boat on the shore. There was no place for us to be on the shore. My father knew of a good long hollow not far from this bay, where we could be out of the wind and the waves on the lake.

As we were taking in our lines with minnows and putting away our lures, fixing the minnows, things in the boat and preparing to move, it came to me to bait my lines with the lizard we caught earlier in the hollow. The line being cast into the wind, here as my father started the motor, the lizard not yet hitting or going into the water, was instantaneously taken by a fish with fish coming out of the water to take the bait. How had the fish known, seen the bait coming in this time, these conditions? Why had the fish hit my line only in this last cast? What was this keen, serendipitous searching that happened with both the fish and the fisherman? We landed the fish in our net in an excitement beyond our understanding. The fish was the good size fighting fish, not the trophy size. We stringered the fish on its own nylon stringer and put it in the bucket of water.

The weather changing cloud was bringing rain not with the lake, not with us. We were getting the wind from the cloud. We could get the rain. It could come anytime. We did not want the rain. We were too far from the boat dock, the cabin. We wanted to find a safe place to be. We had the rain gear if we needed this. We could protect ourselves being in a safe place. We were not in a safe place. The wind picked up, blew the boat around as we moved the boat back to the direction of the long hollow, the safe place. We could not go on this day to the place where the great fish came from time to time. We would not catch the great fish on this day.

As we moved the boat back through the passageway between the island where we had been before and the mountain shoreline into a hollow, we were beginning to be out of

the waves. We could go far back into the hollow, find shelter
from rain and wind and waves. We might could find a place
to fish there. We slowed the boat into a small cove-like place
that had a mountain stream running into the lake. This would
be a good place to fish, as sometimes the bait for the fish
came into the lake here. We fished in this place a short time.
We thought of going far back into the hollow. Across from
this place, the mountain came into the lake creating a point,
this ridge of the mountain extending a little way out into the
bay. The deep water was on both sides. The wind was there.
The waves were there. We weighed these things. We thought
of the point or the calm waters, the challenge or the calm waters. My father thought on these things. It was fun to watch
him think. Maybe he thought the fish would feed on the point
since the lake was being stirred up by the waves and the sun
warming the waters.

The mountain point going into the lake was short. My father must have decided we could get out of the boat there and
maybe build a fire and do the bank fishing while waiting for
the wind to lessen. Further back in the hollow would be the
more calm water but we probably could not be able to find a
place to be out of the boat. We needed to be out of the boat,
to eat some food. We also could watch what this wind was
doing to the water on the bay. We might decide to go back to
the cabin and too, the fishing might be good.

The point to where we were going was quite rocky, no soil
or clay whatsoever. The water level was still down for winter
pool and there were nice, flat places to be. It would be a flat
place to be and off the boat. Several still green cedar trees
grew in the rocks on the shore and down from the point toward
the hollow, willow trees were growing in the lake. High upon

the point on the top of the rock cliffs on the deepest waterside of the point stood a giant, tall cedar tree. It stood atop the rock cliff side of the point as being on a precipice overlooking the lake bay, the lake. It was difficult to understand how such a tree could live so long, be so huge in the place where it was located. It must have begun in good mountain soil and sand, its roots deep in the mountain long before the lake came. Now it was strong, quiet, meditative in its place. It would be a nice place to see, be up close. We would go there to see.

We came to the shore of this point on its more shallow side. Over the years the waves from the lake had broken up shell rock into fine, very small shell particles, leaving a soft, somewhat flat area onto which we could pull the boat onto the shore, leaving the motor end of the boat in the deep water. It would be a good place for the boat to be, should the wind and waves pound the boat onto the shore. Also, too, it would be good for us in the fishing, eating our food, and taking care of things. We tied off our fish stringers over the back of the boat into the deep water. They would be in water a good time now. Only the one big fish we had caught early this morning was struggling for its life. We always tried to keep the fish alive until we were ready to clean them. We got out of the boat our fishing gear, our food, our tackle boxes, our bag of dry clothes, things we needed. We changed the water in the minnow buckets and set these on the shore out of where the waves could turn them over if they had been tied to the boat. The minnows in our buckets lived well on this day. We had only lost a few in the fishing.

Up onto the shore a ways from where we had pulled the boat, another cedar tree had continued to grow and be strong in the rock crevices of the shoreline. The tree would be covered by the lake in summer pool. It was dying from this, but for now it was a good place for us to tie off the rope from the boat. It would hold and steady the boat in its place. We wondered about this tree, how it could hold onto its life, strength, so long in such a harsh place with no source of soil, nourishment we could see.

The wind that had forced us to this place on the lake began to be less. It took on different character, not of apprehension or anxiety but one of invitation. It slowed, it moved away from us. The wind was still there. We could see in a limited way what the wind was doing in the bay waters. We knew, too, the wind of this day could be doing things in the bay area that we could not see. The white caps, the turning over water was still there. We did not desire to cross the bay area. The lessening wind took away the cold or chill in the day. We wanted to stay and fish in this place. The bank fishing was desirous, a yearning to be off the rough waters, and off the boat.

We viewed the areas on the point to see the best places to fish. The bay area side of the point was very deep, straight down, as though a rock cliff was there, and this rock cliff continued beneath the water. We could not see what the rock cliff did under the water. The river was beneath the water there. It was fascinating, mysterious to think of a river being down there once before. What was it like down there? Did the water still move there? Did the fish still go down that deep? What fish or turtles were there? Maybe there were giant rocks there beneath the water. It was enchanting, alarming, fearful and exciting to be looking into the deep waters. It was a kind of a mixing up, turning over of emotions, feelings, thoughts to a trembling in my body. I almost wanted to go down there and be with the river, the places unseen. I wanted to dive from the rock cliff near to this point into these waters.

This was not to be this day in this time. In the years to come, being inquisitive and thoughtful, I would wonder if the man I was seeing in the mountains around this lake ever came here to this place. Did he scale the rock cliff shore with the deep water below? Did he dive from high places into the water? Did he come here in the evenings to prepare his food with wood fires? Did he sit watching the big light leave the day? Or stay here in the night to reflect on the lesser lights? Did he sleep here on these rock shores? I did not know.

On this day I did not look long into the water. It was not good to see the fish we sought to catch. We had seen the fish before and sought to catch these. This had not worked. We did not want to catch the fish we saw. We did not know why. Maybe we felt an unfair advantage over the fish. Maybe in catching the fish we wanted to be equals. Maybe if the fish saw us the fish would be fearful. Did we want the fish to be without fear? Did we desire our contest with the fish to be within ourselves and not with the fish? What was this desire? A small tree was on the deep side of the point; this would be a good place to tie off a rod.

The extension of the point slightly to the left side gradually began to be the deep water. Many large shell rocks were here, good places for the small fish and the crayfish to be, and this was maybe, routinely, where the big fish would come searching for food. We would put two lines here.

Looking out from the point on the left side back toward the hollow, the water was shallower. Small willow trees grew here, just above the surface and beneath the water. This too was a good place for the bait fish and for this fish to come. It would be difficult to catch and land the fish here in this brushy water. We would put out two lines here, one line sort of into the brush and the other not so close. The waves still came into and around the point.

We wanted a fire.

We wanted to sit down to kind of just be with this place.

We wanted to heat, warm our food.

We needed to eat, nourish our bodies from the day.

We did not know how long we would be here.

It would be good to have plenty of wood.

We could not start the fishing until we could stay with our lines.

On the shoreline between the water and where the mountain began, a long dead cedar stump was in kind of a level place, a good place to start and build a fire. It was away from water and not close to the woods.

The walk to gather firewood, having been in the boat so long, was good for us. We needed, desired the walking. We walked away from the point toward the long hollow. The lake, still being winter pool, made the shoreline easy to walk. The shoreline was abundant with driftwood and there were other cedar stumps should we need these. We knew we could have plenty of firewood should we have to wait out the weather for a long time. A good distance from the point an old road came into the lake. It made for a nice level place. Maybe we could come back someday and camp here. The road was nice to see. We did not know where the lake had started in the mountains nor where it had gone once before. I wondered if I, or a man, could come to this place on the lake by walking? The road enticed us; we had to go see. Walking we saw no indications of the road being used in a long time. Certainly no vehicles now traveled this road.

We had no time to follow this road too far. We were hungry. We wanted to be with the fishing. Going back down the road to the point, my father saw what appeared to be an old trail going into the woods. Maybe it was an animal trail? Maybe for someone it once had been a regular walking trail. We did not know. We had to go this way to see what was there. It would be only a little trouble to go this way back to the point, a little trouble would be nothing.

In this walk we came upon suddenly, in an unexpected way, something someone had done here in the woods. A rock sculpture had been constructed and placed in the root system of an oak tree. The tree was early in this life of an oak tree. Most of the rocks were pointed, tapered to extended ends going in many directions with those in the middle ascending higher into spirals going upward, reaching high as though they were petitioning, entreating, making a request. The rocks were different in kind, source, and only a few of those we had seen around or in the vicinity of the lake. On the tops of the spiral, laid flat, were rocks that looked like people, animals, or images unknown. These had been carved, cut to rest, teetering in place. The rocks displayed together as a whole erected an image of something emerging to come into existence.

Gathered around this structure was a collection of what looked like found things from around the lake. Things of little or no value. A drinking cup was here that had five holes drilled in the bottom so liquid could not be contained there. Had this cup once contained the liquids of addiction? Had this been a cup from which someone had drunk and died? We did not know the meanings from what we were seeing.

We were awestruck, astonished to see this structure here in the woods. What was the meaning of this? Who had done this? Had this been done by the man who lived on the lake that no one ever knew lived on the lake? When had this work been done? From where had he brought the rocks; were there other rock sculptures built in other places around this lake? What other things, works had come into the imagination of this man? We could not know the answers to these questions. We could only be grateful to have been here and privileged to see this creation.

We had to leave this place.

We could not contain, stay too long with this experience.

We only belonged here in this place a short time.

We returned to the point to do what we had to do.

When we had come to this point again, the place had taken on a different character. It was no longer just a good place to be, a place to catch the fish, a place to rest and wait in the weather. It became a place of silence, memory, reflection, meditation, thoughts, searching for meanings. The place, time, was becoming a kind of second place, a place speaking to me, a place evolving as to intention in my life, a place for celebrating stories, a place of hope and giving to others.

The time of day was beyond a short time after when the big light had been straight up in the sky. We did not have the timepieces, we did not care for these; being with the lake, timepieces seemed or could somehow shorten our time with the fishing. The temperature was another warmth from before. The big light had been coming to the rocks a longer time. The wind still blew, still bringing waves to the shore. The bay was still filled with the white caps. We could almost come out of our on-the-lake warm clothing. We did not want to cross the bay. We could still catch the fish.

We walked around the area of the point to decide the places to cast our lines. We gathered some of the firewood we had found and put near the place for the first. Before building a fire or setting our lines we wondered looking out over, around the bay—a long ways from the cabin.

We wondered.

Were we the only fishermen on the lake?

Were we alone today?

We talked on this.

It was a little eerie.

Was the known fisherman fishing today,

Fishing a way we did not know?

Had the thin old woman and wiry old man come on the lake today?

We knew that in their turn they had been fishing in the windy and most difficult of days.

Maybe these days were behind them now.

We wanted them to be on the lake.

We did not know.

Later in my life I would wonder on the fishing of the thin old woman and the wiry old man. Why did they do the fishing together as much for so long a time? How did they do the fishing? What secrets had they learned? What were the challenges that kept them in the fishing? Did they ever leave their boat and the fishing to find places of privacy, nakedness, intimacy and passion? Did they bring blankets, pillows staying through the night for both the fishing and their times together? Surely they had done this as there were many places for such to be.

We were anxious and excited to put out our fishing lines. We put out five lines, one on the rock cliff side into the deep water, two lines directly off the point and two lines to the left side of the point toward the hollow. We weighted our lines to help get the minnows to go down to the deeper water; otherwise, we knew the minnows would swim back to the shore where they would be safe from the fish. The securing of the lines was difficult with the winds blowing. We baited four lines with our largest minnows and one line with the crayfish given to us by the old woman who sold the minnows. We put the crayfish line near the willow trees that grew under the water. It was a difficult and good place for the line to be placed. Good catches had been made in such places, but many more almost good catches were lost.

Soon after setting our lines, tying them off or securing the rods with rocks, the starting, building of our fire was easy. The winds blew the flames, dry driftwood was in flames soon and the hard cedar would create a sustaining heat and warmth. We wanted to build up a fire to a blaze. We desired to see a good fire. We wanted the fire to last. We built up the fire more than what was needed. We wanted to allow the fire to go down, to be smaller, to still be hot and warm. We soon heard the sounds of the popping cedar wood sending hot ashes in the air. The fire was in a place where the winds blew the ashes toward the bay area and the deep waters. The fire was in a good and safe place away from going into the woods.

We sat on the wind-coming side of the fire. We stayed out of the smoke and cedar-popping cinders, a little too warm on one side and a little too less than warm on the other side. It was the way it was. We knew we could watch our fishing lines. We had the bottled soft drinks, the containers of drinking water. The coffee was gone. We heated leftovers wrapped in the aluminum foil from the dinner the night before. We had roasted duck given to us by the boat dock owner, fish given to us by the thin old woman and the wiry old man; there too were the potatoes and carrots and cornbread. And, of course, we had the small cans of sausage, the pork and beans. We could open these if we wanted to do this. The peanut butter was always with us. We feasted and ate with our hands and gave no attention to the dirt, the smell of fish, minnows, night crawlers of all the other things we had handled. Our hunger was our feast. The memory, experience of this time of eating together is burned into my mind—not to be forgotten.

Sitting there with the fire, we were thinking. What were my brother and sister doing? What was my mother doing? Were they okay with us being gone so long? We talked on these things. My father said he and my mother had talked about us trying to fish long into the day. Probably my brother and sister did not think about us all that much. They were too young to think much on our being in any danger. I did not sense any danger. We were fine; the weather now was the more pleasant. We had to move away from the fire. It was burned down and hot. We were able to come out of our heavy clothes.

I was thinking of the fishing, the possibilities. My father was thinking. I was watching him think. I did not know what he was thinking, did not have an intuition. I just knew I was watching him think. It was not about the fishing or even the place and what we were doing. It was about something else. Maybe he was thinking about his job, the earning of the money, being the father, being the husband. Maybe he was thinking about his childhood, his family of birth. Maybe he was thinking about something personal that he wanted to share but did not know how to share what was on his mind. Maybe it was the meaning of his life, what he wanted to be and do a way that he could not be or do? Maybe he was thinking of the death that would one day come to him. I did not know what he was thinking this day at this time. I did not know how to think on many things. I only knew that I was just learning to think. I did sense my father's thinking was different than many others. I sensed he thought long on things, had many questions. I sensed others did little thinking, had many answers. You could tell something was missing from their talking and knowing so much, so many answers.

I did not talk with my father about watching him think. He did not talk with me about his thinking. I did not talk with him about my thinking. He did not talk with me about watching me think. I wanted to know more about his thinking. Maybe he wanted to know more about my thinking. We did not understand well how this could happen.

Only after many years from this day, becoming a young man and committing with a woman to living together and having children was I able to hope to understand my father's thoughts; and this was to be in the time a few years before it would be time for my father's death, and this too would continue throughout that time of now to my own anticipation of dying. So, is how it was and so is how it is.

Memories, thoughts come to me now.

In the year before the year my father was to die, I went to visit him to see how he was doing. I knew his health was failing. It was time to be with him as much as possible. No prognosis was in place from physicians as to when he might die, it was just time to think on this.

My father asked me, "Do you think I am dying soon?" I answered, "Yes." My answer was with the least of hesitation; so direct, immediate that such surprised me and unnerved my father. We did not expect or want this recognition. It simply happened. Why had he asked me this question? Why did he not tell me his thoughts? He seemed a bit frightened to hear this from me. He said nothing of his fear or his thoughts on dying, or his dying.

He told me only that he had loved and been faithful to my mother all the years of their marriage, that he wanted me to know this, that this was important for me and for him. Why had my father told me this? Was this an apology for the arguments, difficulties my father and mother had in their marriage? Was this a request of forgiveness, a sense for redemption for the injury happening in my youth to my brother and sister? These times were painful, harmful. As my father talked of loving my mother, how important she was to him, I knew the many good things in their life together and in our family. My mother and father loved each other. They had been loving and taken good care of us children. My father in this time was not remorseful, repentant, nor in sorrow as he knew he and my mother loved each other; that they had in a continuing way learned and done what love is. He knew that love was hard work, that it changes, is not always the same, that he and my mother had done this as well as others. He knew that I knew this. This, these thoughts, feelings were simply important for him to share with me.

In the last visit to be with my father and mother, death was certain to be soon. My mother was quiet, in peace, in comfort watching, caring, and not frightened or in anxiety; they had talked. My father was anxious, nervous, restless;

there was something unfinished in his life, something unset-
tling as though he had one more thing to do, one more thing
to figure out. What was his pain in his dying time? Was it an
unfinished desire? Dream in his life? Was it something he
wanted to say, hear? I did not know, could not figure out his
difficulty. Maybe the pain was the difficulty of dying. Maybe
his unrest was the pain in his going away body or the pain
leaving his body. I did not know. Maybe he was considering
a last thought, choice, act of courage.

Maybe in this visit a significant thought, choice, division
happened as I was to see and remember a story from my father's youth. The story became poignant, meaningful to me
when outside the double glass doors and onto the porch a
snow had fallen. A squirrel was there, doing its multiplicities
of activities. My father's talk, attention to anything, every-
one else stopped. He was there with the squirrel outside those
glass doors. He was in a special place, time of memory. I was
in the story. Something was happening in him. It is not possible for me to write what I saw in my father's fair eyes. A
smile was there, something beyond contentment and peace;
maybe it was a relinquishment to a last choice, action.

Closer to the time of my father dying, he was hospital-
ized for evaluation, diagnosis, treatments for his failing health
due to cardio-pulmonary difficulties; the hospital happened to
have been one of a specific religious faith, denomination. It
was a religion of different persuasion from his youth, different from his adult experience with matters of religion. While
visiting my father following this hospital time, he found it
important to tell me of the good, attentive care given to him.
A nurse who wore a distinctive religious style of clothing was
very kind, thoughtful, caring, and competent. He liked her.

She had a way of being with him, his pain, his suffering. He trusted her. He had liked her questions about faith, matters of belief, common questions in religious thought. She had told him she did want, desire to answer his questions; she did not want to persuade him to her faith, that she could ask someone else to talk with him if he so desired. He did not want this. He did not need the answers to his questions. It was only that he was curious about a faith that would help a person be as this woman was with him. He wanted only answers from someone who had the answer.

My father was neither a believer nor a non-believer in matters of faith nor did he go to the services of worship, prayer, and traditions. He was not a proponent of any authoritative perspective; was leery, suspect and sometimes disdained of those who spoke to know all answers relying on exclusive authorities. He enjoyed songs, music, stories from various faiths, cultures. He carried sayings, stories with him in his mind for speaking what occurred to him to be in the right time. He loved telling jokes and using humor to say his meanings. I think he loved most the use of questions to say or to understand his thought. If my father had a belief or thought to be written down, maybe it would have been that his life was a gift to share with and for others, that his joy was to tell stories and work with his hands, to claim no authority in any manner or about anything.

A brief time after the last seeing of my father, early during the month spring comes, a snowstorm came in other mountains where I lived with the woman in my life and our children. The snow was significant, deep, covering everything, filling the woods and weighing down trees. The snowstorm had come in the eve before and the early hours of the day of worship.

The snow, the early morning was inviting. We, the woman and our children, went into the woods trudging, wrestling, romping, playing in multiple ways in the snow. We pulled down mini snowstorms from the branches, built snow structures, did the snowball things, saw, encountered visual images, creations never seen before that would never be seen again.

And, then, on returning from our play, I called my mother and father on the talking box to tell mom of our morning, what we had done. My mother answered. I could tell she had something to say she could not say. I asked to speak to my father. She said, "He is gone." I knew. Then she explained, he had died in the hospital in the morning hours.

My father's work career had been in personnel management, labor relations, and workman's compensation, so too had been the work in my life. Without formal education or extensive knowledge from classes, from books, my father knew and had learned much of medicine, law, and employment benefits. He knew all the dynamics of the illness, diseases in his body. He knew what the medicines did and did not do regarding his life. He knew that if he died after a certain date, his wife would not be paid from an employer-paid life insurance. He did not take his life; he withheld his medications to allow his death to happen. I never told my mother what had happened.

Soon the time of funeral and burial came. Visiting with my mother in this time, my mother told me that my father had told her early in the week he was to die; he felt he would die on Friday or Sunday. He died on Sunday. She was asking, how could he have known this? She did not know. I did not know. Later while visiting in this time, looking through some notes made by my father I understood what had happened. The notes were not specific and did not say what was in his mind. He had not intentionally left these notes. The notes were not for anyone to see. My knowing was just something I figured out. I know.

Now, I wonder in this time?

Now, I ask in this day?

Maybe when our death comes all our failures, differences and ill-will toward others, self-interests, arrogance, negative frames, habits of mind and what we have not liked about ourselves and even the great wrongs we have done go into the universe to form new stars, planets, life forms, to even more solar systems; and all that is left of us is the good we have intended, done, left in stories, creations, work within ourselves and being helpful to others. Are we forgiven in, by, with our death?

* * *

Though, on this day my father did not die. He stood up from where we had been with the fire. I stood up too. We were tall here. We looked onto the lake, the bay was full of the white caps of waves, the waves to the point were to the deep side of the point, not directly to the point. There was sort of a lull with the waves onto the point. The sky was blue with the high fast-moving clouds, some parts sparse, some parts full. We know this could change, could be anything. My father said the baits were probably too close to the shore, we should check them. We did this, rebaited the lines, four with the minnows, one with the night crawlers for maybe the small fish or the whiskered fish. The line with the crayfish had been hung up on something and we had tried to break the line. Maybe great fish had taken the crayfish line to the tree beneath the water or to the hidden place within and beneath the rocks.

We did not know. We used our biggest minnows to maybe catch the biggest fish. The lines were easier to cast this time. The fish could be there now; they seemed to hit the minnows most often soon after they were in the water scurrying for safety, security.

My father knelt on the shore where the point went furthest into the water. We could see how the rocks went into water; they had the color of the light from the big light and such cast shadows of the waves. There seemed to be movement beneath the water with the light and the shadows. My father turned over some rocks looking for a crayfish to move. He said that even if we saw or found a crayfish here, he laughed, amused with himself, knowing he would not be able to catch the crayfish in the deep water, the advantage was with the crayfish here. A little way from my father I gathered handfuls of the small shell rocks looking for shells or collections to take back home with me to where we lived in the other mountains.

I watched my father kneeling as he seemed to have paused in what he was doing. He was looking around, wondering, wandering in his mind as though he was not here but in another place in another time. He was quiet; I did not know how to know. I did not want to disturb him; I did though. I walked over to where he was, distracted from where he had been; he smiled, turned over a rock, a crayfish mound. We laughed with delight.

The big light had been long enough now in the day to warm the rocks beneath the water, to cause the water around those to sort of enliven and to entice the crayfish, the smallest minnows to move and to stir the fish to feed. Our minnows had not been in the water long enough to find a place to hide. Our lines began to move. It seemed as though all our lines were moving at the same time. We did not know which line to gather first. The first line I gathered was relatively easy to land. It was on the bank not able to get back in the water. The next line I gathered was open, a good deal of line had been taken. It maybe was a big fish. I was frightened of this. Would it be able to be landed? The fight was on. I did not know for sure what to do. All of this seemed to happen so quickly and also to be so long. My father landed his fish and another fish. My fish was still in the water. He let it swim out some from the point into the deep water. After a time as the fish had tired, we were able to get the fish close to the point into the deep part of the water. With the net we were able to land this fish. This fish would not be eaten. It was a trophy size fish to be mounted. It was a brown fighting fish, like the great fish. It was not the great fish. Two of these other fish were the brown fighting fish, one of the others was the big mouth fighting fish. We would eat these fish. We had caught good fish on this day.

As we had caught those fish and shortly thereafter, the wind, the weather began to change. The wind came more from the west, the direction the big light was going, and the wind was stronger and the white caps of the waves more direct to the point where we were. The clouds were moving away, the blue of the sky was majestic with big light now beginning to be another warmth. It was a good time to be where we were and we thought about my mother, brother, and sister. They were probably having a good time in and around the cabin. They would be gathering the firewood, planning our dinner, climbing trees and playing in the woods. They probably never expected us to be back to the cabin soon. They did not know what the wind was doing to the water or that we were so far onto the lake, though, probably mother had feared we had gone too far onto the lake. We wanted to return to the cabin. We had caught enough of the fish for this day and we wanted to leave for home, although it would not be wise as the wind had just begun to be far too strong and waves could be much bigger out in the center of the bay. We could not go down the rock cliffs and stay near to these as the waves were moving in that direction and it was not good to ride with the waves in the little boat, it was always best to go slow into the waves and to be patient against the waves. We wanted to wait and give the wind some time to be less. This sometimes happened especially if a storm was not to come. Against us though was the truth. The afternoon wind usually stays longer. The morning wind sometimes leaves soon. The wind, the weather was unending, anything could happen. We worked with the firewood we had gathered, put on another cedar stump, our biggest cedar stump. It would keep the fire longer.

We talked about, wondered whether or not the thin old woman and the wiry old man were still on the lake. It would be nice to see them, to have companions here on this day, such would help us with our secret fears, here on the lake alone. Our desire to see them was not to happen. If they had fished this day it would have been mid-morning. They would have gone back to their home earlier in the day. They would not have come into the winds not as we had seen them.

We knew favorite places the thin old woman and wiry old man fished; they would not have to cross the big bay and at most they would have only crossed the shortest section of the bay. We would not see them on this day. We, or at least I, wanted them to see the fish we had caught this day.

I wondered.

We wondered.

We talked.

Should we tell the thin old woman, the wiry old man or anyone at the boat dock or anyone at any time where and how we caught the fish? It was of legend, or tradition, a sacred secret honored by fishermen not to tell exactly where fish were caught. I understood this, felt proud to have this secret. We would not tell. I held in my heart, being a boy, that back in the other mountains I would tell my friends and those who would listen to all the details; after all, they probably would never come to this lake to fish.

* * *

Long after the time of this day, in truth being shortly after my father died, I returned to this lake in grief to fish and be in/ with this place again. And here on this point I was to catch a similar trophy size brown fighting fish. And it is also true that on this day the famous fisherman from this lake was fishing on the same day. I wondered where he was fishing, what he was catching. I wanted to see him, show him my fish, and tell a few of our stories; that was not to be. I secretly hoped he would hear of the fish I had caught.

And too, it is true that as a father I would bring my two adult sons here and tell them the stories of this day; and while here they also would do well with the fishing and even catch their trophy size brown fish. It was a day when I simply did not want to leave the lake, a passionate love had grasped me—this place, the day, was simply too extraordinary to not share with others.

So now, in coming to this time of telling these stories, the catching of these fish, the time, the day, the place are true without any embellishment or any fictitious details; so, why depart from the legend or tradition revered and honored by fishermen? Is it that the same fish cannot be caught again? Is it to help others tell and share their own stories? Is there a healing in telling truth in stories? Is there another sacredness in finding, telling the truth in our stories? I do not know, though it is true I am honored to be able to tell these stories.

Is the search for the truth of things the great fish? I am inviting other fishermen to find this place, to find and tell stories of their own places. Maybe only a few fishermen will be able to find this place, be able to find their place, their stories.

* * *

With the new, different, more prominent winds coming—having caught our fish and put out our lines again, we became less interested in the fishing. We began preparing ourselves to stay with the lake. We could not cross the bay. The big light was well past the straight up in the sky. The winds were bringing sparse, fast-moving clouds into the sky. We still had the blue skies, though this could change. We knew a storm could come that evening and night could come. The winds brought on a kind of intermittent cold. We put on our lake and earlier day clothes, pulled the boat a little onto the shore so waves would not move the boat too much against the rocks.

The winds now were beginning to change again as though there were several winds coming, at least a wind from where the big light was going and another wind from the direction that brings the warm, hard rains; the rains with the great noises and flashing lights. The winds seemed to be clashing against each other, turning around within and against each other. These winds were creating a different kind of turbulence with the lake.

The waves began to change, they now were a certain treacherous danger. We had to stay with this place. We had no choice.

We had not seen another boat on the lake this day; neither the houseboats, the big fast boats, nor the fast speeding fishing boats. As we were preparing for the changing weather, the winds died down and we began to see other boats on the lake, some around the bay coming out of the hollow where we had been in the morning, a boat here and another there. We saw one boat able, substantial enough to travel through and with the bay waters. There had been other fishermen on the lake this day, this inspired us and made us feel not so alone. These fishermen were going back to their boat docks, back to their cabins, homes. We were pleased to see them, happy for them. We had fear, intuition. They had fear, intuition. The weather was creating for them choices, decisions, things to do or not to do. It was a time of no argument, to only do what is next.

In this time, two fishermen came in a fast speeding fishing boat. They pulled in close to the point to talk with us. They had been fishing all day. They had caught no fish. We talked with them. We showed them our fish. They were impressed, pleased for us. They wondered if we would be all right in the weather. We thanked them, said we thought we were safe. We would stay here 'til the weather passed. These men were at loss for where they were on the lake; they needed directions to a known boat dock. We knew this boat dock, the way to go. We told them to go between the mountains on our left and the island on the right, more to their right side of the lake and stay with the right side 'til they got close to the dam; they would see the boat dock. They were happy to know the way. They had confidence we knew what we were saying. We knew they could be all right in their boat.

There was another story here. These men, though jovial, affable, courteous, friendly in their manner, had been drinking this day from the brown bottles and from this did not know where they were on the lake. As a boy I knew this. I had learned this with my father. He, too, when in other mountains, his place of work and normal life, drank from the brown bottle. He never drank from the bottles when we were here with the fishing, the lake. My father too knew these men were lost in what they were doing. As a boy this day I was angered by the brown bottles, their drinking did not belong with the fishing. As the two fishermen left in their boat, I admonished these men for their drinking. I do not remember my thoughts, nor what I said. I just remember the happening.

* * *

Years later in my life in talking with my father about this fishing day, this time on the lake, I would tell him my desire to write stories of these times, this day. As we talked, he said that it would be good to write such things. He said he also would have liked to do such things, but such was not his gift. He had a question for me.

Will you write about the two fishermen drinking, being lost and not able to find their way on this lake? When I could not say what I would do, or say the truth why, we allowed the question, the answer to be uncertain without clarity. We both knew why. So, as best I am able here is what is true.

We, my father and I, both of us drank from the brown bottles, the opaque bottles, the clear bottles, the fancy bottles, the kegs, and the cans. The stories around such are many and varied, some good, some bad and not so good, and some just normal good times. The whats of the stories are not so important as the whys. We drank from the bottles because we desired to think different, feel different, be different. We did not like how we were, how others were, how things were. We did not know how to adapt, be adept, be a part of life with others. We could not find a way to honesty, transparency, being alive without fear. We could not find a way to say what we wanted to say, feel what we felt without guilt or shame, do what we wanted to do without hurting others. We thought and maybe somewhat the drink helped. We, my father and I, in time found ways for endings and the end of the potions for happiness.

Why did we, why do we need to feel, think, be different? What were the whys? What are the whys? Were they distances with parents? Were they complaints between parents? Were they absent parents? Were they abuses in our childhood? Were they extreme financial problems? The whys and whats could go on, on, and on.

What are all the other efforts to think, feel, be different? What are the whats that make us feel, think, be different? Are they money, power, prestige? Are they success in employment? The answers, the remedies could go on, and on.

What is the searching?

As the two fishermen left into the wind, the waves, the winds began to be more intense, bringing clouds to take away any remaining blue skies. The day soon would be complete cloud cover. The winds offered no promise they would subside; extreme weather was coming. The waves in the bay and coming to the point had become more than rough, with them turning over white caps, they were turbulent waters with unknowns as to what they would do or what power was in their movement. We hoped the other two fishermen would be all right.

The winds were too difficult for the fishing, so we began to prepare for worse weather, maybe even a storm and a rain. We put up our fishing gear, secured the stringing of fish over the back of the boat further into the water, pulled the boat more onto the shore. We covered various things with a small tarp. We built up our fire with the larger pieces of wood, the wind blew the fire well. The fire became big, strong, too hot to stand or be close to. The winds were not cold; the temperature was good. Should the rains converge, we had rain gear that wears like a tent over your head and body. We had brought dry clothing in bags should we need them.

We wanted to have more firewood should we have to stay into and through the night. It too would be good for the fish to be strong should the people from the boat dock come looking for us, they would be able to see our location easily and that would be a good thing. The people at the boat dock knew we were capable, but still they could come looking for us. We were not frightened, we were just being careful, thorough and thoughtful in our place. We went down the shoreline and easily gathered more firewood. We put some under rock ledges near us to keep the wood dry even in the rains. This wood could keep a fire going even in the rains. We had one cedar stump that if we decided to use this it would burn through the night. We stoked hot coals together in the center of the fire. We thought, talked, and laughed together that it would be good if we had coal from the other mountains for our fire. We did not; it was fun though to think on this.

We could not stay with the fire, it was too much, too hot. We wanted to be away from fire, allow it to burn down, be less. We had little or nothing to do. We were a bit unnerved.

We went up from the shore, away from the point to the place where the giant cedar tree sat near the edge of the rock cliffs. We could see out better over the bay from this place. We took with us to this place the last of food we had brought. We only had pieces of meat from the previous day's dinner, a couple of apples, a can of the little sausages, bread and peanut butter. The coffee had long been gone. We had a couple of soft drinks and of course our thermos water containers. We ate plenty of the bread and peanut butter. The food was good, enough to fill us. The place of the cedar tree was a good place to be.

Beneath the giant cedar tree both my father and I were in thought, a kind of meditation, an infectious thought. We were not talking but kind of in the same place, the same way. We did not need to talk, we needed to be patient, wait, listen. And as we were here, the winds began to subside. The fast-moving winds were moving out of the area. The waves on the lake lessening in the turbulence, still with the white caps and rough water but not looking so treacherous. A lull was happening in the winds. What was this? What did this mean? Was this an indication, invitation for us to prepare to leave in the boat? We still had plenty of daytime from the big light. The skies still had coming and going areas of blue, though to our area more cloud cover was coming. What were those coming clouds? We did not know. We only knew the changing weather seemed to be without notice to tell us what was to happen.

With the changing wind we decided to walk further up the ridgeline at the mountains; being higher we could see better the bay area, a little more of what was happening out in the bay. My father told me that he did not think it wise to cross in the middle of the bay. We might could go in the boat along the rock cliff shoreline, staying close to the shore till we could get into the shallow water areas where there were good places to be on banks closer to the boat dock. We might could do this.

Was the lull in the winds a test for us? Was the lull a deception as to what was really happening? Could the winds start back up? Would they be in the same directions? Did the lull mean another storm was coming? What kind of storm? We did not know. We felt we must do something, make a choice, go somewhere, make something happen. At least we must decide. We decided we would wait with the weather. We would not try to outguess the weather. We would be patient. We would not challenge the weather. We would allow the wind, weather, waves to tell us what to do and how we should meet its demands.

What would we do as we waited? We would look for shelter in the woods. We went back to the point to check our things, put wood on our fire. Maybe we could find branches, or limbs or something to help us build a shelter with our tarp near the fire. Maybe we would have to stay here through the night. We did not know. Going back to the point was easy. All our things were in good places, shape. We could go look for shelter.

Back to and on the point, the winds began to increase, though this time the winds were different; they were more low down to the lake. The wind had picked up in a quick time, almost as though it had come from nowhere. The wind was not the steady wind, not the straight wind; it was a wind with stops and starts over again, that had turns and turning arounds. These winds were stronger winds creating intermediate gusts around us, within us. The winds blowing onto the point threw our fire around in many directions; up the big cedar stump and down to the point and the shore. The fire was not to be too close. The wind blew our boat on the shore. We feared that the boat could be blown from the shore. We put things in the boat to weigh it down and to be sure it would not be blown into the lake. We did not want this. These winds, though perplexing and somewhat frightening had a warmth to them making us feel strong; there were exhilarating gusts inviting us to be, to stay with them. We did not know these winds. They were something we had not seen before.

The waves on the lake were turbulent, coming onto the shore, moving rocks and making sounds of water falling, splashing, moving rocks against each other. The sounds were rough, not the lapping, but the crashing sounds. The waves on the lake were a continuous display of white caps, treacherous water everywhere; not a good place now on this day for any boat to be. We no longer looked for boats to be in any place we could see.

We left the point to find shelter going along the shoreline to the road that went into the mountains. We would go up that road to look for a place to be. The cloud cover now was low, close to the ground, so close; we could almost touch the clouds. The cloud cover was staid and steady as if to stay with us, be with us for a long time. Within the cloud covering, one elongated cloud appeared to be within what was happening. It was sort of different; apart from the cloud cover. It was dark, black, thick, long in its distance, strange. It was imposing, foreshadowing; probably it had a great deal of rain. Was this cloud coming to the lake? Would it come to us? What did it hold? What did it bring? Was the cloud going to envelope the lake? It was and could be a darkened time when the very least of the big light could be seen. It could be almost the total dark; a storm within storms?

As we had come to and were going up the road into the mountains we began to see flashes of the lightning in the clouds. We began to hear the rumbling sounds. The flashes of lightning were in the clouds around the big dark cloud. Would flashes of lightning come from the giant dark cloud? Would the flashes of lightning soon be all around, all over the lake? We had seen this before on and around the lake but always from the safety of the cabin. We had never been on the lake as this was coming to be. Something was happening and now, whatever it was, it was near certain to come to us.

The walk up the mountain road was fast to do, we were soon well away from the lakeshore. The sounds of the coming storm or storms were with the winds in the trees. The sounds of thunder were first a distance from each other, then they were more frequent. Those with the lightning were as such we could not tell which thunder followed which lightning; then it began to be as thunder and lightning in hostile conflict with each other, making loud, harsh, angry noises. Those were as being in war against one another.

We stopped in the way of the road. We stopped to see and be in this. We were perplexed. We were bewildered with less than good choices then the rain came. We knew the rain was coming, we expected this; but we did not know the rain would come so hard, so fast, so sudden as to surprise us, put us in an immediate quandary. We left the road to go into the woods toward the lake to find shelter. We did not want to go too far away from the lake.

Into the woods we came upon what may have once been a trail for animals and maybe a path or two for a man. We did not know; it just had a rough trail appearance. We went in this way. It went toward the lake, toward the ridge of the mountains. We came to a place of several great rocks. One of those rocks overlapped several larger rocks creating a sort of cave place. We went to this place. It had plenty of room for us to be out of the rain. We know many of such places in the other mountains where we normally lived. In and around such places were play grounds for the children in the mountains. We were here in a good safe place.

We could see from this place what was going on. We quickly gathered a little firewood for a fire to warm us for a time. The fire was easy to do with small dry pieces of wood being beneath the rocks. This place had good space for us to be. We wondered if this was a place where animals came; had others been here in this place; had the man I had seen on the lake been here; had he or others slept in this place; had there been other fires here? We knew this could be if we had to do this.

In our place with the rocks we were only a short distance from the rock cliff shoreline with the lake. The ridge of the mountain going to a point was also near to us.

We could see through the trees to where the bay waters were on the lake. No wind other than the one that brought the storm was now coming, it was a great strong wind to move along and diminish the sounds and lights of the storming This wind brought pourings of water, so many fallings of water that for a time we could see only a short distance. Was there something breaking up in the heavens, releasing their pain from petitions? Was the rain a kind of renewal? Were there pourings of rain fears, griefs, loses, resolutions of conflicts with us and in this storm? We, my father and I, talked on this rain, what it was? There was something good about a great rain such as this. We knew the storm would run out of water. We knew the storm could not hold enough water to be forever. As we sat here in this good and safe place, a simple bird of the sparrow kind had come here as we. The bird was not threatened by our presence, it too was grateful to be out of the storm.

The pouring rain was to slow then began to stop just as it had started. We were able to see again to the areas around us. The rain with us was near to stop. We could see though a rain was still over the lake. The rain had stopped with us but was still with and over the lake. We wanted to see what the rain, the wind was now doing. We left our place of shelter, going to the ridge of the mountain and edge of the rock cliff overlooking the bay. The rain was staying with and over the lake but was settling the lake; the rough, turning over white caps were gone.

Another different wind was coming; no longer the hard, rough turning around wind; it was a warm sweeping wind coming in up and down layers. It was as if waves of this wind were bringing sheets, waves of rain. One sheet of wind and rain after another as though both the wind and the rain were walking on the water. These, this was sort of a final say for the storm to be gone from the lake. The waters on the lake now were without the waves or any white caps; they had become like the warming winds.

As we were here on the ridge, we knew we could go in the boat, the rain with us was the least. The very least of the light in the day remained with us; maybe the big light had been gone from the horizon during the storm. We knew this dark of the night was soon to come. We were able to see, with what least of light remained, our way down the ridge to return to the point. We did this only to stop for a short time beneath the giant cedar tree. As we were here, the winds and sheets of rain were moving beyond the lake to be with us no more. Maybe the big light had not been beyond the horizon very long; maybe the big light too was moving the storm away from the lake. We did not know. We could not see any signs of the big light in the still cloudy skies. It was time to go in the boat, another wind could come, and another storm could come. We knew sometimes two storms came back to back. We knew too that sometimes storms turned around and came back.

Being again on and with the point, the sounds of water, winds, waves were almost gone and the very least of rain was to us. The rain was soft, almost to non-existent; the sounds were close to silence. In the place of our fires a few hot coals remained from the cedar wood. We stirred these to see the amount of heat, we added a few pieces of wood to establish some flame and a little more heat. We needed a little warmth to change to some warm clothing. We removed our rain gear, took off our fishing hats and hot jackets. We put on warm shirts with hoods and we put back on the rain gear to break wind in the moving boat. As we were doing this, we had gathered a great deal of firewood. We could build up the fire and stay with the lake. We would like to have stayed but this was not the right thing to do. We left the firewood gathered for the next fishermen who would come here to be on this point.

We set our boat back in the water, brought in our stringers of fish on the rope. The early morning large fish had died.

We would gut and clean this fish when we returned to the boat dock. Our other fish were still alive, they would live on their stringers in the buckets of water. We could leave those on stringers at the boat dock. We wanted the people there to see our fish on the next day. We could take pictures with the fast camera and leave them with the boat. We changed the water in our minnow buckets, ordered our things in the boat. We were tired and weary; we were ready for the boat ride home.

As we were in our boat a little offshore, the starting of the old motor was a little challenge, taking patience, timing, pushing the choke for gas and pulling the cord. The motor started in a short time. We let the motor idle for a good time. Once the motor idled well, we knew it would take us to the boat dock.

The time in the day was when the darkness of night had come. We did not know how long the big light had been gone. The departing cloud cover kept away all light. It was dark. We could not see across the bay. We feared to cross the bay for maybe losing our sense of direction and becoming lost. We could follow the rock cliff shoreline to keep our bearings. We could see those rock cliffs. We knew them and we would be in the shallows. From those shallows we knew a place to cross a least section of the bay. Maybe by then, the cloud cover would be going away and we would have light from the lesser light. We would go our way slow to the boat dock. We were comfortable to be in the boat moving away from the point; it had been a good place and even though a place that could not be again, because of the good things that happened for us there, it would remain with us a place to be celebrated again and again.

Though the storm winds and the storm cloud coverings were gone, high in the skies was another cloud cover and another wind. We could not see this; we just sensed, intuited this. We could not see into these night skies, but we felt something going on high in the skies. Maybe a wind was taking another storm to another place? Maybe a wind was taking away all the clouds? Maybe we could see the night skies again on this day?

The lake was settled now; only the trailing winds from the storm were still with us. The waves on the lake were major white caps. We would be traveling with the waves now, not against them. We moved away from the point only a little with the bay. We had to keep in sight the rock cliff shoreline. This would be best in the night. We knew we could follow the rock cliff shoreline to the shallow waters. We were content though the bay frightened us now with a different kind of fear than we had had in the morning.

We had gone a good ways from the point; I looked to the mountain ridge from where we had come from being in the storm. The ridge was distinguishable from the mountains and the night skies. Our eyes had adjusted to the dark night. I saw movement there going down the ridgeline toward the point. Two figures of beings unlike anything I had ever seen. As I looked closer, closer, so close as to listen, feel my heart beating. One being looked like maybe a tall, lanky man and the other appeared to be a wild animal of some kind. I wondered in the terror a joy. Could I be seeing the man who lived on this lake that no one ever knew lived on this lake? Was he alive? Did he have an animal as a companion? Had he seen and known that we were there? What was this vision, this imagination coming to me? Was I just seeing things? I told my father what I was seeing. He looked. He could not see what I was seeing. In a little time, no longer could I. This imagination was gone.

A lull in time, distance happened. We had moved well away from the point, a little into the bay area. We were still a distance from the shallows. Now in the dark of night, we had another sense of comfort. I looked into the darkness back to the point; a fire was there. I wanted to see the fire, I part way stood up, pointed to my father, told him what I was seeing. He looked, too. He turned to me and smiled. It was good to see the fire on the point a long distance away. We wondered what was happening? Had wind stoked the fire again? Was the being I had seen gone there to start up the fire again? Was there a companionship there between the two beings I had seen? Was there dancing in, around with the fire? Was there laughter, joy?

What was coming from this fire? What was this fire—a meditation, self-reflection, sharing of stories, healing, forgiving, another kind of loving? I wanted to go back to the fire to stay with the lake. My father wanted to go back to the fire. We could not go back, not at this time—not yet. My father moved the boat back close to the rock cliffs. We needed to stay close to the shore 'til we got to the shallows. We now could not see the place of the fire.

My father turned on his running light on the back of the boat. I turned on my running light on the front of the boat. We desired our location to be seen should someone be coming on the lake to find us. The running lights would not bother our vision in the night. We now knew well our way to the boat dock.

My father moved the boat slow toward the shallow waters. I, the boy, lay down in the bow of the boat and went into a sleep as though to relinquish the day to the little time when we would be back to the boat dock. A dream came in my sleep as though time was nonexistent and I was carried away to many times and places.

The standing hills stood quiet, peering into water on shorelines.

The striped fighting fishes chased the minnows in the bays, camping and swimming, places came a many.

The evening doves were cooing goodnights.

The sounds of the owl were in the night.

The crows were doing their talk.

The sea gulls were coming in winter skies.

The buzzards were hovering over everything and then there was a momentary flight of the eagle.

And in the dream, I was present and flying too.

And I did not desire to wake from the dream nor to come down from the skies.

It was great joy to be one with these creations.

The sounds of water, waves against the boat and the faster movement of the boat woke me from this sleep. We had gone through the long time in the shallow waters. My father said as I awoke, "We are crossing the bay." This was the very short place to cross the bay. The waves in the water here now were not the very rough ones. We could not see those well in the night. We were not going against the waves, not going with the waves. The waves were coming to the sides of the boat; though difficult to maneuver, we were not in danger. We only had a short way to go. We could see the big island across this section of the bay that would give us shelter from the waves and could take us out of the winds.

Crossing the bay area, unknown flashings of light came into the dark cloud skies. They were here, there, multiple places in a close together area. We had no idea what we were seeing. We, exhausted from the day, felt alarm; anything unknown to us initiated in us an anxiety, a fear. Our apprehension, trepidation, misgivings also enticed, invited us to see, to know what was going on. My father slowed the boat, we turned off our running lights. We came to an almost stopping of our boat. What was happening in the clouds? Was a happening coming through the clouds? Was a happening occurring beyond the clouds? Was this happening coming to us, to where we could see? Would this happening remain unknown to us? What unknown event was happening? Would this happening harm us? We could not know what was or what came to be. The glimmers, the scintillating light became intense. We knew only the unknown, what was happening, what would be was beyond our control; we could only gather our fear, our no fear, respond, continue our way. We could go into the unknown, then fear had life, we could be the mystery. The unknowable there for us and against us.

The lightings in the clouds left, were gone as fast, as quick as they had come. We continued our way close to the mountain island; and then, just as we moved closer to a point on the island to go toward the hollow from where we came in the morning, the happenings of the lights occurred for us to see. The complete, finished, lesser light was there in an incident of time. It came without notice, brought to us relief, a kind of joy, a loss of the uneasiness of the dark. The high, fast-moving clouds were dissipating, ending; they were going away. And, too, we felt a different part of the day was gone.

The full lesser light was astonishing to see, it brought light to everywhere around us. We were enthralled by this and seeing this, as though we were one with what was in our sight. It was as though being there in shadows on this circular sphere, climbing on rock cliffs, walking on sands, being and doing things there. The sense of presence of being so with this sight was mysterious, a mystical moment taking me to the place, places I was yet to be. High clouds still in the skies, this light intermittent as such might surely take us to the end of this day.

The winds here gone now, they were going somewhere else and not to be with us anymore on this day. These no longer challenged us, troubled us. Moving by and with the camping place, the lesser light illuminated the areas where I desired to come for the camping. I was to imagine what was to be—this was who I was and desired to be. In the unseen, unknown in my life was a dream, a potential, a possibility.

I am haunted, inspired, enchanted by earth, water, skies, winds; knowing, intuiting not only the beginning of any existence, but also the support and shaping of meanings in my life. These as creation, entities other than my mind, body, and soul are an existence other than my being. The waters of this material, observable world, even my life itself remains unknown, mysterious and maybe even so into infinity. What I am able to know is my love, joy with mountain streams, creeks, rivers, lakes, and of course, the colors and majesty of the vast universe. I know too that whatever beauty in earth, water, skies, winds I am able to conjure in my imagination is not able to represent existence, creation. I am not these, I love these. I would like to be as these, creating and sustaining life. I love being a part of these. Like water, being almost silent, working with earth, rocks, quiet, giving something to the existence of life. Without notice sometimes I am with creation, experiencing the essence of life coming in memories, stories want to stay around and not be erased; and I am drawn to share stories with others so all our stories may be so honored, celebrated.

* * *

A time came when another story happened here with this lake; having become a young man, loving a woman and having brought more children into life, we came here for the camping. We did not have the means for the cabins, nor the big or the fast boats. We had the desire to be on the lake. In those times we rented a fishing boat, the least expensive, and made several trips getting ourselves, camping gear, foods, and fishing things to this the camping place. We, though somewhat anxious without roads, calling boxes, conveniences, adapted well and loved being on the lake. These times were days of summer, swimming, fishing, laying in sun on rafts, walking and building things on shores, teaching our children the swimming, the enjoyments of nature. Friends came with us, brought their fast boat; we learned and did the skiing. We had great times together with the day fishing, the night fishing and of course, preparing and eating of foods.

One time, one night when no one else was here camping, we, the woman I loved and I, awoke from sleep, the late evening and early night sleep. We had gone to bed early in our tents, our daughter in her tent our two sons in their tent. The love and those times together in the evening had been wonderful. I did not know why we awoke. We fumbled on clothes.

We kissed a little, held, hugged each other. We wanted to be outside the tent. Our shoes were outside the tent. We wandered around the camping area for a time. Our children were quiet, sound in sleep. We ate things from our foods. We were enjoying one another.

We were in the middle of the night; the night was warm. The night was clear with not the lesser light nor any clouds in the skies; there were only the multitudes of the least lights. The lake was calm with no wind, no waves, the lake was quiet. We walked to the shore of lake and as we were there, a light appeared in the water. How could there be a light in the water? We walked to various places on the shoreline trying to see the source of light. We did not know. We were troubled by the light. We, in some fear, even imagined something sinister or harmful to us. We desired to go see what the light was. We could not swim to the light it was too far. We did not want to go in the boat and disturb, alarm our children. Anyway, the light seemed to move as we moved. What was the light? And, then, in being a time with the light we saw, it was a reflection of one of the least lights. We were calmed; the lake became more calm, smooth, like a mirror reflecting many, many stars more than we could see. The light out there, the light with us, the light within us was all the same.

We were invited. We took off our shoes, our clothes, left them on the shore. We desired to swim in these waters with the lights and then as we wanted, needed, we swam away from the camping place across a cove to a time place of intimacy and privacy. We, the light, the lights within us were together. This time was exquisite. We swam back to our campsite. We dried with a damp towel. We gathered and dressed in our clothes. We found together dry sleeping clothes. We slept warm. We woke together early. We prepared, on a wood fire, a breakfast of bacon, eggs, onions, and leftover fish and, too, we made toast with bread on sticks.

And then, in another time years beyond these stories, as we lived in the other mountains, the woman I loved began to go away. A long-suffering, neurological, chronic, disabling disease came within her body—it changed her gait, walking; it impaired her sense of balance; it impaired her dexterity; it affected her ability to speak so no words could be said; it shut down her swallowing food to the necessity of a tube in her stomach; it almost shot down her smile 'til she laid still until no longer able to breathe.

Before death, even with our sufferings, we sometimes went to a lake near us in the other mountains. One warm, summer day we were to be in a place where an old road went far into and beneath the waters. It was a place where people gathered for swimming, fishing, doing the picnics and cooking out. A cove was there for sunbathing on air rafts, being on rocks in water, playing in, with soft shoreline rocks, building rock castles. We had done those things here. On the day I am sharing, we went into the lake on the road, I pushed the wheelchair and the woman I love smiling, enjoying this time.

I remember the big light shining into the water with the wheelchair, creating glistenings and reflections of lights, attracted the little fighting fish. These came to nibble on light, white legs, excited and searching for food. This was an exciting frenzy of activity, fun to see. A smile came to us. This woman said, or tried to say, with unclear, almost unspoken words. She called my name and said, "Look, see all the little fighting fishes." These words have stayed with me to never leave. (In spite of the woman's pain and loss of so many things, she was able to experience interest and joy in others and things.)

We all go away, or do we? We all flinch from doing things, or do we? Is the work of a man greater than the man? Is the work of the creator greater than the creator? What remains? Do our stories remain to stay long? Does our work remain to go on? Are our stories greater than the stories? Are all our stories of value? Are we to listen, value, honor the stories of others? Does the truth remain? What is the truth? Does the truth answer the questions? Are the questions the truth? Are we all to answer our own questions and honor the quest of others in their searchings? How shall we do this? Are we to do, leave something for life, the earth, the water, the skies, the winds and movements of time?

* * *

The light from the lesser light was gone now with the comings and goings of intermittent clouds, the one now being of size and duration. We were well into the hollow of the lake, the one with the creek from where we had come in the morning. We were around a bend in the hollow to being able to see in the distance the lights on the boat dock. The lake now was calm and the winds were gone. We had a way to go to reach the signal buoy. We could soon be safe from the challenges of the day. We wondered where my mother, my brother, and sister would be waiting for us. Would they be in the cabin or had they come to the boat dock? Surely they would be worried, concerned for us by now. We had been on the lake a very long time. They would be well; we would be well when we saw each other.

The cloud cover was staying with us, the darkness was with us. We were back with the rock shore on one side and clay rocks on the other shore. Would I be able to come back to this lake again? Would I be able to fish here again? Would I be able to come, search for things done by the man on the lake? Had he been there as I had seen him? Had he built houses, towns, cities, transportation in clay banks? Were there many rock sculptures around this lake? Had he had many places to live? Had he died here? Did anyone else know or know of this man? Who was he? What were the many things he had done? I wanted to know why he came, what he had learned. Had he left writings of some kind? Had he left writings in caves? Would he still be here when I returned?

We could see well now the lights on the boat dock, only three or four of the single bulbs. As we were seeing the lights our vision, perceptions were beginning to change, to adapt to normal life. We would soon be back to the usual activities, experiences. We would need the lights. I was not sure I wanted to go back to those lights. I had another awareness, another awakening. This day had changed me in ways I did not yet know; it had set me on another path. We could see now the signal buoy. We slowed the boat into still waters. We could see no one was at the boat dock. Our family was waiting for us in the cabin.

We had come now to and by the signal buoy into boat dock waters. Soon, we would be able to see into the lake where the little fish swam. We would pay no attention to these. The anticipation of the fishing would be gone. We were exhausted. We still had to somewhat order the things in the boat, put away the trash, arrange the fishing gear and prepare ourselves for the walk back up the mountain to the cabin. We could do this, but that was mostly all we could do. The lights of the boat dock welcomed us. We turned off our running lights. We were having an experience of peace; the difficulties of the day were resolved. We slowed the boat to almost idle, used our paddles into our boat slip.

Being with the boat dock, almost home now, almost to the cabin was as though all that had never happened, all that had happened in this day and all that would happen in the future was present in this moment. We did not understand this, though somehow we knew this was true. We had two minnows left in our buckets. One minnow was in my father's bucket. One minnow was in my bucket. My father reached with his left hand into his minnow bucket, he gathered the minnow left from this day and he released the minnow into the lake. I, too, released the minnow left in my bucket into the lake.

We put the fish we had caught on their stingers over the side of the boat. We had taken care to keep them alive. They would be fine in the cold water in the night. We would come back in the next morning and take the minnow buckets with us. We would not fish on the next day. We would be too tired; though in the next day we would go to the home of the old woman who sold the minnows and we would tell her some of our stories. She would be happy. We would tell her we only needed a few minnows as our times of fishing here this time were only another day or so.

She would tell us her excitement to see us the next time… and how she would keep fishing and walking in the creeks….

Finis: David Marion Herndon

January 02, 2013

CPSIA information can be obtained
at www.ICGtesting.com
Printed in the USA
LVHW031917260720
661581LV00004B/411

9 781952 714993